Endorsements

As Pastor Clint Ritchie so accurately states, "The family is God's way of preserving faith in him to the next generation." In this book, he shows how important the family altar is in preserving the family itself. Listen to his practical and proven suggestions that will strengthen the family and strengthen the faith. We so need this encouragement today!

Dr. Frank Page
CEO of the Southern Baptist Convention
Nashville, Tennessee

As a beneficiary of a family altar, I was delighted to see the book that Dr. Ritchie has written. Knowing him to be a down-to-earth, godly, and compassionate pastor gave me hope that finally someone had written something to help us rebuild one of the most important institutions in Christendom ... the Family Altar. This book instructed and blessed me. What a great message for floundering families!

Dr. Emil Turner
Retired, Executive Director of the Arkansas Baptist State Convention

God has established three institutions: the church, the home, and human government. All three of these institutions, because of their priority and value, are worth preserving and strengthening. It should be noted, however, that due to their importance and value, all three are under constant attack by forces, both internal and external. Clint Richie offers some long-overdue and helpful insights into how the church can support families in their mutually supportive roles. Every pastor, children's worker, and parent will appreciate the foundational and practical information on the place of a family altar. I pray that this book will stimulate you to reestablish the family altar as a priority in the homes around you.

Dr. Mark Tolbert
Professor of Preaching and Pastoral Ministry
Director of the Doctor of Ministry Program
New Orleans Baptist Theological Seminary

Traveling in evangelistic ministry almost 30 years, I have seen all stages of family interaction both inside and outside the walls of the church. With the precision of a surgeon's scalpel, Dr. Ritchie dissects the cause of today's family struggles. With clarity he goes step by step in diagnosing the issues and along with it, offers solid biblical examples of how to move forward to be the family that God desires and to aid parents, even includes a year's Bible study. This book, with God's guidance, will convict parents and create a new, sold-out generation for His glory.

Rev. John Yates
John Yates Ministry, LLC
Enterprise, Alabama

Rebuilding
the
Family Altar

Dr. Clint Ritchie

WESTBOW
PRESS®
A DIVISION OF THOMAS NELSON
& ZONDERVAN

WestBow Press books may be ordered through booksellers or by contacting:

WestBow Press
A Division of Thomas Nelson & Zondervan
1663 Liberty Drive
Bloomington, IN 47403
www.westbowpress.com
1 (866) 928-1240

ISBN: 978-1-4908-8834-7 (sc)
ISBN: 978-1-4908-8835-4 (e)

Print information available on the last page.

WestBow Press rev. date: 03/22/2016

To Jennifer, the love of my life

Contents

Foreword...ix

Preface xi

Chapter 1   The Use of the Altar..1

Chapter 2   The Abandoned Altar...5

Chapter 3   The Role of the Church 9

Chapter 4   Biblical Foundation for the Family Altar.....14

Chapter 5   Parental Influence...18

Chapter 6   Clearing the Hurdles......................................24

Chapter 7   The Discipline of Prayer.................................30

Chapter 8   The Discipline of Bible Study........................40

Chapter 9   The Discipline of Praise 48

Chapter 10 Other Family Worship Disciplines................52

Chapter 11 Start!..59

Appendix 1: Weekly Devotionals......................................61

Appendix 2: One Mother's Story 119

Foreword

The need for this type of book is long overdue. This is not a popular teaching in our churches today. People need to know and come to an understanding of what is important in our homes and families. Everything has taken the place of God in our homes, which allows for Satan to find a foothold and destroy the family altar, something that many see in disrepair.

Dr. Ritchie has taken the time to develop a much-needed view of establishing the altar in the home. Families may not look the same, but there is no substitute for the family values in the home. This culture is crying out daily to see a change in what is happening in the home. Tolerance and a cultural shift have created a need to see God placed back in the family where He belongs. Dr. Ritchie has taken something that has been lost and brought back awareness and clarity to developing this shift back to the church. Family ministry has been lost when we just drop kids off, and they are in youth and children ministry locations. This book helps us understand the need to bring God back into the home. I think every parent needs to read this book. Dr. Ritchie understands the difficulty in this process, and he seeks to help develop strategy for your home.

Doug Compton
Evangelist
Doug Compton Ministries
Paragould, Arkansas

Preface

My service in churches, first as a youth minister for three years and for the past ten years as a pastor, has allowed me to see many families at their worst. Parents have shared with me the struggles they have with their children and the burden they have for God to do a work in their lives. In their relationships with their children, they have talked, yelled, cried, disciplined, and attempted other forms of motivation, only to find themselves in my office, the school principal's office, a counselor's office, or a police department, wondering where they went wrong.

After witnessing the brokenness of many parents, I attempted to talk to their children and found they have distanced themselves from their parents and their concerns. They are numb to the conversations, pleas, and discipline; they want to be left alone. Those who are toward the end of their high school years can often tell me exactly how many days remain before they can move out of the house and get away from their parents. Still other parents struggle when their children begin college and quit demonstrating the importance of their faith.

When these instances occur, blame is passed back and forth between the parents and children. While there is usually enough fault to go around, there is a failure to recognize the situation as a spiritual attack. Satan loves to destroy the family. Divorce, rebellious children, debt, time restraints, and many other outside influences are used to bring destruction. But he also uses parents who ignore their children's spiritual development until it is too late.

In my personal discussions with parents struggling with their children, I regularly find parents admitting their shortcomings in developing their children spiritually. They admit they focused on the children receiving a strong education, winning at sports, and having the best "stuff." But "I took them to church" was not enough spiritually.

Instances like these described motivated me to stress ministry to families in my ministry. However, when I became a parent in October 2006, God placed a continual reminder of the importance of children's spiritual development, as well as their interest in spiritual matters. I have watched my children, now ages seven and three, develop a desire to have the Bible read to them, memorize Scripture verses, and talk about spiritual matters. The innocence of a child has shown me God places this desire into each of us, and it is one's parents who either feed it or let it starve to death.

I was blessed to grow up in a Christian home that modeled active church participation. However, it was not until I was in college that I was discipled. I was serving as a youth minister and majoring in Christian ministries, yet I was lacking the spiritual maturity I needed. I sought the help of a campus minister to assist me through the *MasterLife* curriculum to foster my spiritual development. A personal ministry goal is to properly disciple members of the churches I pastor, and I hold firmly to the conviction that the home is the best place for discipleship to occur. I also hold the conviction that parents, specifically fathers, are accountable for the spiritual training they provide, or do not provide, to their children.

The conclusions in this book are based on my pastoral experience and the research performed for the doctor of ministry degree at New Orleans Baptist Theological Seminary. The project report, "Equipping Selected Married Couples with Children of First Baptist Church, Hampton, Arkansas, in Family Worship Disciplines," undergirds this book.

This project would not have been possible without the continual support of my wife, Jennifer. I thank God daily for placing her in my life. The joy of my children, Addison and Whitley, serves as a reminder of the importance of practicing the principles in this book.

I am also thankful for the encouragement from Dr. Mark Tolbert, Dr. Harold Mosley, and Dr. Chris Turner of New Orleans Baptist Theological Seminary for planting the idea of this book.

Lastly, I am thankful for the churches I have served. Bethel Station Baptist Church in Paragould, Arkansas; Swifton Baptist Church in Swifton, Arkansas; and First Baptist Church in Hampton, Arkansas, have opened their lives to me, given me opportunities to minister, and laid the foundation for this work. I look forward to impacting families in First Baptist Church of Yazoo City, Mississippi, as I begin serving as their pastor. The couples from Hampton First Baptist Church that participated in the original work made a huge investment, for which I am eternally grateful.

Chapter 1

The Use of the Altar

People of every culture commemorate special events in particular ways. They celebrate birthdays by giving gifts and eating birthday cake, they observe holidays with family and close friends at cookouts, and they honor retirements with receptions. Still other events require parades, special programs, or other forms of commemoration not used daily. When a special event occurs, people feel the ingrained need to put plans in place to ensure participants will celebrate and remember the event.

The Old Testament is full of similar occasions in which the people of God commemorated events through the building of altars. Altar building was always directed toward the God of Israel. The people built altars during times of joy, times of sorrow, and times of victory and defeat. Sometimes they built altars as signs of repentance or as reminders of God's faithfulness. After they built the altars, they offered sacrifices of animals, grain, fruit, wine, or incense on them.

The first altar in the Bible was the one Noah built after the flood. Imagine the joy that filled Noah's heart as he walked onto dry land from the ark after surviving the flood! As his family and the animals disembarked from the ark, Noah was moved to worship God for His faithfulness and provision, so he built an altar.

When Abraham arrived at the land God sent him to occupy, he

1

built an altar, serving as a symbol of his possession of the land, an accomplishment granted by God. He built other altars to call on the name of the Lord. At one point, God told him to build an altar on which to sacrifice his son, Isaac. Isaac would later become an altar builder himself at Beersheba, after the Lord appeared to him and reconfirmed the promise given to Abraham: "I will bless you and will increase the number of your descendants for the sake of my servant Abraham" (Genesis 26:24).

Moses constructed an altar and named it Jehovah-Nissi, meaning, "The Lord, our banner," in celebration of military victory. Before entering battle, Gideon built an altar after God called him to lead the people of God against the Midianites—the same people from whom he was hiding in fear. David built an altar at the threshing floor of Araunah to stop the plague God put on the people as a result of David's pride in counting the fighting men.

The altars became the places where the people connected to God. The people built them out of reverence and the desire to worship, expressing their dependence and thanksgiving. The building of an altar was an emotionally charged event. God worked, and the people responded. It took time to build the altar. The people needed to gather the materials, and the physical labor they exerted often came after a time when their physical energy was exhausted.

Through the atoning sacrifice of Jesus on the cross and the Holy Spirit's indwelling in the lives of Christians, we now build altars not out of sticks and stones but out of the essence of our hearts. Through our personal relationships with Jesus, we have the altars of our hearts. New Testament altar building can be described as an act of worship from the heart that flows out of a desire to approach God, recognizing His sovereignty and holiness. The sacrifice each of us now offers is one of praise and a contrite heart.

Just like the patriarchs of the faith, we experience times of victory when we express thanksgiving to Him on the altars of our hearts. When He leads us to places we have never been, we recognize His provision. After coming through a storm, the altars of our hearts express humility before the faithfulness of God.

We sometimes know difficulties in which we must search deep within to muster the strength to utter waning prayers or praises. Yet the desire to acknowledge God and give Him the praise He is due leads the struggling soul to offer sacrifice on the altar of the heart.

New Testament Christians are deeply familiar with another altar—the family altar. The family altar affords a time and place when a family gathers and offers a sacrifice on the collective altar of their hearts. Traditionally, the family altar is not a physical structure but the regular time of the family coming together with the sole purpose of acknowledging and responding to God.

One can see the family altar in the family that rises from the table to join together in thanking God for His many blessings, each family member giving testimony to God's protection that day. It is pictured in the family of the Great Depression that gathers in hunger to feed on God's Word. The father who gathers his children to teach them the stories of God's provision after coming home from his last day of work at the factory uses a family altar. Teenagers use these altars as they share with their parents the struggles they face to conform at school; their parents' tears for their children plead for the strength of God to come upon them. A mother gathering her preschool children to teach them the words to "Jesus Loves Me," a simple yet profound truth, builds a family altar. The family altar also comes to life when a child shares about a classmate whose home burned, parents divorced, grandparent died, or some other tragedy, and the family pauses to pray for the classmate and discusses ways in which the child can minister to his or her friend.

Just as Old Testament altars were nothing elaborate, the family altar does not have to be a time of lengthy prayers or deep study. The value is found in the family coming together to focus on and praise God.

In the Old Testament, the people of Israel built altars using what was available. The simplest were the earthen altars, made of either mud-brick or a raised, roughly shaped mound of dirt. The most commonly mentioned altars in the Bible were made of stones, either a single large stone or several stacked together. People simply used what they had or what was readily available. This practice enabled them to build the altars immediately, rather than delaying the projects in order to gather materials.

The family altar uses what the family's members have available— their home. When a family gathers at its altar, members do not have to seek a special place. Instead, they meet together where they already are. They may sit together on the floor, around the kitchen table, or in a specifically designed place. If the family had to get into the car, determine a place, and then drive to it, they would seldom, if ever, gather at the altar. When the family gathers in the home, God reminds each person of His provision of God, giving them another reason to respond to Him.

Chapter 2

The Abandoned Altar

Throughout the Old Testament, altars were places where God and His people ratified their covenants with each other. An altar was to be a place in which a legally binding agreement between people and God occurred and where they made solemn promises. It was a place where the holiness of God met with the sinfulness of humanity, a place where people could right their relationships with God through atoning sacrifices.

The altar was so significant that God instructed Moses to build one as part of the furnishings in the tabernacle. The tabernacle, the altar, and the priest who served there had to be consecrated and atoned for according to God's divine order. The consecration of Aaron and his sons as priests required blood from the altar and anointing oil be sprinkled on them and their garments. After Aaron and his sons were consecrated, they followed God's instructions to purify the altar so it would be holy. Each day for seven days, they sacrificed a bull as a sin offering to make atonement for the altar. They were also instructed to anoint the altar to consecrate it. From that point on, whatever touched the altar had to be holy. At the entrance of the tabernacle, sin and thanksgiving offerings were to be made daily before the Lord. This was all part of the preparation needed to sanctify the tabernacle, so the glory of God could reside there (Exodus 29:43).

All these requirements for the care of the altar and those who sacrificed upon it give an idea of God's holiness. The altar was God's provision for the people to remain in right standing with Him. Unfortunately, due to human corruption, the altar became a place where people invoked and worshipped false gods.

In 1 Kings 12:28–29, the altar of Bethel, which had been a holy place of meeting between God and Abraham, and later Jacob, was turned into a place where people performed sacrifices to false gods. Because God would not remain silent, He sent a prophet to prophesy against the altar (1 Kings 13:1–13). The prophet foretold the days when Josiah would utterly destroy the false altars people erected at Bethel. God fulfilled this prophetic word in 2 Kings 23:15, when He used Josiah to destroy the high places of false worship Jeroboam established.

In 1 Kings 18, Elijah challenges the prophets of Baal on Mount Carmel. The people believed they could follow both God and Baal, so Elijah calls the people to choose who they would serve. After the prophets of Baal received no response from their god, the Lord demonstrated His power by sending fire from heaven to consume the sacrifice Elijah prepared and the water poured upon the altar. It is important to note that before Elijah could offer the sacrifice and before God would display His glory and power, Elijah had to repair the Lord's altar that the people had torn down (1 Kings 18:30).

Throughout the Old Testament, some altars were destroyed and left in ruins. Others were used for sacrifices to false gods. The holy was made unholy. The meeting place with God was abandoned.

A similar destruction has happened to the family altar. Families no longer gather at the altar. God desires to meet with the family, but the meeting place within the home is abandoned. There is no specific time when the family gathers to acknowledge God and respond to Him.

This destruction of the family altar has been steady in the last fifty to sixty years, at least. It was once common practice for a family to eat together, with no one leaving the table until given permission from the parents, usually the father. After the food was eaten, the parents would discuss with their children how the day went. The parents might discuss among themselves struggles at work or financial difficulties the family faced. The discussions would regularly lead to how God would provide or how He provided in the past. The family might remain at the table or move to another location, but the parents would take their children to the family altar. Again, it was not necessarily a physical place but a time when they would meet with God as a family. A Bible story might be shared and prayers offered. And there were times when the father might act like a preacher, challenging his children on the Scriptures that had been read. Some adults testify it was in this setting they learned to read at an early age.

For the most part, my generation is only familiar with the described scenario by seeing it on television or hearing about it from grandparents. It is now the norm for a family to eat "on the run," rarely enjoying a meal at the family table. In a time where both parents work outside the home, evenings are filled with ensuring homework is completed, baths are taken, and each bed is occupied as quickly and early as possible. Extracurricular activities such as school programs, ball games, and the like only take away from the time at home.

My research shows that when a family gets to spend time at home without an agenda, they all go their own ways. It is a time for Dad to catch up on the sports and business sections of the paper. Mom usually has housework that is screaming for her attention, while the children have their favorite shows to watch or websites to visit. Some parents commented that when they are all home in the same room together, each person is still wrapped up in his or her own individual activity. The increased availability of electronics has only accelerated this problem. All family members can be in the same room, each playing on an electronic device, oblivious to what the others are doing.

While the time at home is limited, parents who have been challenged to rebuild their family altars have conveyed it is possible. It is a matter of priorities. One family committed to use the time at the dinner table. Another said the time right before bed, when the kids were winding down, was the best for them. Another family found the time spent commuting in the car each day was best used when they turned off the radio, and one of the riders read and discussed a Scripture passage. This family ends the commute with prayer before leaving the car.

Unlike the Old Testament commands, there are no specifics on how to build your family altar, only that it be built and used. Just like Elijah rebuilt the altar before he could call on the Lord, parents must make concerted efforts to make the necessary changes in order to lead their family to worship together. The world has a great need for men and women of faith to step up like Elijah and lead their children to proclaim, "The Lord—He is God! The Lord—He is God!" (1 Kings 18:39).

Pagan altars were abundant through the Old Testament as people followed the example of the God-fearers and built altars to worship the gods they served. This remains a battle today. Competition for the altar of our heart is fierce. One does not have to look far to see the allure of pleasure. Pagan altars are plentiful. The need remains for the people of God to use their altar to worship God.

We can learn much from Abram about building altars. At Shechem, Abram encountered God and reacted by altar-building. Next, he journeyed to a place between Bethel and Ai, where he built an altar in his desire to meet with God. This became a pattern for his life. He later returned to this altar between Bethel and Ai and again called on the name of the Lord. Abram continually built altars in response to God's call (as in Shechem) or to call on God (as in Ai) before he continued his journey. God was central to whatever Abram did, and the altars appeared wherever he went.

The altar is the place of guidance for one's journeys. Do not go far without building an altar. As often as necessary, revisit it!

One final thought about rebuilding the family altar. In the Old Testament, when altars were used, the times were good. When altars were broken down, neglected, and forgotten, times were not good. God has not changed, and neither has His desire to meet with His people. The condition of your family will emulate the condition of your family's altar.

Chapter 3

The Role of the Church

Has the Church Helped Destroy the Family Altar?

This chapter begins with a personal note regarding my feelings toward the church. I love the church! The church is the bride of Christ. I have given my life to serving the Lord and His people through the church. This chapter will not be one that berates the church. Just as I will not tolerate anyone speaking harmfully toward my bride, I believe God will not remain silent when people speak harmfully and act maliciously toward His bride. Please understand the words in this chapter are written with great humility and caution.

The lack of presence and poor condition of the family altar in the homes of Christians reflect the family's church. A church's ministry to families has focused on getting the parents to bring their children to church. Churches celebrate the arrival of families, especially ones whose children have attended special services or children's services, and the parents begin to attend. Once a family attends church together, they are designated "a Christian family." What happens the other six days of the week?

Churches spend significant resources on their ministries to children and teenagers. They plan fun activities. Buildings and rooms are built or renovated with the intention of reaching. They train their teachers how to keep the attention of the class. Many even employ someone to focus on ministering to these age groups. None of these things are bad, as each occurred in the churches where I have served. The problem is this has led to the creation of this mind-set of parents: "I take my children to church so that they learn about God."

I regularly see parents leave one church for another church because, "They have more for my children." As a parent, I completely understand the desire for your children to attend a church they enjoy. It makes a parent's job easier. I also understand parents want their children to be in church with other children. But changing churches does not alleviate parents' responsibility to teach their children about the Lord and His ways. God did not give this command to the church; He gave it to parents.

The other extreme in regard to this issue are the parents who do not attend church because they believe they can do a better job educating their children spiritually. While this is may appear honorable since the parents accept their responsibility, we were created by God to live in the community of faith with each other. Isolating ourselves from other believers contradicts God's plan for His children.

A key to building the family altar is the church and family working together. Parents attend church with their children to worship and study God's Word with others, while the children have a class or ministry that gives them the same opportunity. In some churches, this may all occur together. What happens when the services are over? It is essential that churches equip parents to lead their families throughout the week.

Curriculum companies have started to see this importance, as many of them are creating age-appropriate curriculum for the entire family. Mom and Dad have the same Sunday school lesson as their children and teenagers, creating opportunities for the parents to dialogue further about the topic during family worship time. Other children's curriculum supplies a sheet for the children to take home that explains to the parents what was taught and how they can reinforce the material in the coming week.

Churches need to "get it" like the curriculum companies. Worship and study are not just things that happen on Sunday. It is the beginning of a weeklong process of spiritual growth through responding to God's Word and His work.

Much attention has been given to the numbers of older teens and young adults who leave the church. Most research concludes that 80 percent of those who were raised with regular church attendance as part of their lives will drop out of church after high school. People much wiser than I have attempted to conclude why this exodus occurs. I believe it is due to two main reasons, both related to family worship.

The first reason has to do with the division between church and home. Children grow up going to church faithfully. They sit with their parents each week, seeing them smile at everyone and saying all the right things. Parents make sure their children do what is expected of them in the service, and everyone is happy. Then the service is over, and the parents do not appear for another week. The only other mention of God might be in a mealtime prayer, but the smile is missing, and the parents are completely different people. Going to church each Sunday did not change anything, so when the children are no longer under the influence of their parents, they quit the church. They do not want the faith of their parents.

While parents may not realize their deficiency, I am convinced if the church equipped the parents and challenged them to take their actions and what they learn on Sundays to the other days of the week, churches would not see the absence of young adults, like they do today. When their parents' faith does not change their daily life, why should their children want any part of it?

Children need to hear their parents read the Bible to them, uncovering the truths of God's Word. They need parents to pray with them, celebrating the faithfulness of God to hear and answer. They need to hear how God provides strength in times of difficulty. They need parents to tell them how personal disobedience cost them. This can occur at the family altar, but as long as it is abandoned and parents are content to only take their children to church, the church will continue to lose generations.

The second main reason we see young people leave the church is that they were never prepared for life. An accusatory finger has been pointed to colleges, blaming them for teaching material that is adversarial to Christianity, along with offering many experiences students have never had within the church. But the Barna Group's research determined many young Christians dissociate from their church before they encounter the college environment. In fact, many are emotionally disconnected from church before their sixteenth birthday.[1]

David Kinnaman, president of the Barna Group, states that the core of the problem is the lack of preparing young Christians for life beyond the youth group. His research shows only a small minority of young Christians have been taught to think about matters of faith, calling, and culture. "Fewer than one out of five have any idea how the Bible ought to inform their scholastic and professional interests. Most lack adult mentors or meaningful friendships with older Christians who can guide them through the inevitable questions that arise during the course of their studies … The university setting … exposes the shallow-faith problem of many young disciples."[2]

Parents have left the spiritual development of their children to the church, and each church has done the best it can. Yet when the children become teenagers and later adults, they are not prepared for added temptations and responsibilities. The family altar is a great place to prepare children for the world. It takes the church and parents working together to develop disciples who can be sent out to impact the world for the cause of Christ.

Parents are the primary influencers in the life of a child.[3] While many churches have an effective children's ministry that sees children and teenagers learn of Christ and grow in spiritual maturity, nothing can replace the spiritual influence of parents. The time children and teenagers are involved in the ministry of their church does not compare to the amount of time they are with their parents. T. B. Maston states

1 "Five Myths about Young Adult Church Dropouts." *www.barna.org/teens-next-gen-articles/534-five-myths-about-young-adult-church-dropouts?q=teens+leaving+church*.
2 Ibid.
3 Connie Neal, *Walking Talk in Babylon: Raising Children to be Godly and Wise in a Perilous World* (Colorado Springs, CO: Waterbrook Press, 2003), 25.

that the home, "is a more important institution for law and order than the state, and even a more basically important religious institution than the church. There is no surer barometer of the condition of the culture than the sickness or health of its families. As the home goes, so goes everything else: school, church, and civilization itself."[4]

George Barna's research concludes that people are most likely to make a spiritual decision regarding Christ before the age of twelve. His research also indicates the belief systems of children are set by the time they are thirteen.[5] The childhood years are the crucial time to shape one's spiritual persona, and churches and parents must work together.

---

4 T. B. Maston, *The Bible and Family Relations* (Nashville: Broadman, 1983), 57.
5 George Barna, *Transforming Children into Spiritual Champions* (Ventura, CA: Regal Books, 2003), 34.

Chapter 4

Biblical Foundation for the Family Altar

The idea of a family altar and parental spiritual influence is nothing new, as it is the plan of God. He has ordained the family as the foundational institution of human society. The familial relationship provides the opportunity for individuals to learn to live godly lives. Diana Garland notes family is the channel through which ministry takes place and provides the world with a graphic portrayal of God.[6] The more-effective families are, in loving one another, the clearer the image of God.

Scripture gives specific roles to the family. Wives are commanded to submit to their husbands because the husband is the head of the household.[7] Husbands are to love their wives sacrificially, and the picture of the marriage relationship is found in the relationship between Christ and the church.[8] Children are commanded to obey their parents,[9] and fathers are called not to exasperate or embitter their children.[10]

The role of the parents in the spiritual education of their children is

---

6 Diana R. Garland, *Family Ministry: A Comprehensive Guide* (Downers Grove, IL: IVP, 1999), 326.

7 Eph. 5:22–23; Col. 3:18.

8 Eph. 5:25–32; Col. 3:19.

9 Eph. 6:1–3; Col. 3:20.

10 Eph. 6:4; Col. 3:21.

often overlooked. Parents have four main roles regarding their children: encourage, nurture, discipline, and instruct.[11] The Old Testament supports the view parents are to teach their children spiritual and moral values and to lead them, through consistent lifestyle example and loving discipline, to make choices based on biblical truth. Deuteronomy 6:4–9 is a command for parents to pursue vigorously the intentional development of a heart for God in their children.

> Hear, O Israel: The Lord our God, the Lord is one. Love the Lord your God with all your heart and with all your soul and with all your strength. These commandments that I give you today are to be on your hearts. Impress them on your children. Talk about them when you sit at home and when you walk along the road, when you lie down and when you get up. Tie them as symbols on your hands and bind them on your foreheads. Write them on the doorframes of your houses and on your gates.

The rapid sequence of the verbs brings understanding to the force of the advice: impress ... talk about them ... tie them ... bind them ... write them.[12] Among the people of God, fathers considered their role in spiritual training an honor and were committed to fulfilling the responsibility.

The family is God's way of preserving faith in Him to the next generation. God commanded Abraham to "direct his children and his household after him to keep the way of the Lord by doing what is right and just."[13] God instructed Moses for parents to teach God's commands to their children, so their days may be many.[14] God warned His people that failure to train their children would result in a generation that does not live with the purpose of God in mind and, therefore, will face the

---

11 Tony Evans, "The Parent's Role in the Home," *The Alternative View* (December 2004): 2–3.

12 Christopher Wright, *New International Biblical Commentary: Deuteronomy* (Peabody, MA: Hendrickson, 1996), 100.

13 Gen. 18:19.

14 Deut. 11:19–21.

consequences.[15] The failure of one generation to follow God can impact multiple generations.[16] Parents who fail to teach their children the ways of God are bringing judgment upon themselves and their children.

Mary and Joseph were entrusted with the responsibility of raising Jesus. They fed Him, taught Him to speak, and helped Him to stand. God could have chosen to bring Jesus to earth fully grown. Instead, He was born as a helpless infant to young parents divinely called to nurture Him toward His calling. The calling for parents has not changed, and the call to impart to children the ways of God, "is just as much a response to the call of God as the response to leave everything behind to take up Jesus' cross."[17]

Parents are the God-ordained spiritual leaders of the family. Following God's plan for parenting does not ensure that parenting will be easier, only that the parents will be obedient to God's command and that other generations will have the opportunity to respond to His call on their lives.

The family environment is ideal for dealing with the problem of sin and coming to salvation. Family relationships present parents with opportunities to teach their children through example and practice. Jesus' ministry was focused on the goal of redeeming people and equipping them to be proclaimers of God's redemptive power. No institution is better prepared for implementing this strategy than the family. The most significant impact a Christian can make is leading someone to accept Jesus' offer of salvation, and parents have the unique position to direct their children toward this decision, laying the foundation for a fruitful life.

God's grace is available for all humankind to accept or reject.[18] Everyone makes a choice to accept or reject salvation, and parents have the opportunity to mold their children toward the disposition to accept Christ when His offer of salvation is made available through the Holy Spirit's conviction.

---

[15] Deut. 6.
[16] Ex. 20:5; Num. 14:18.
[17] Garland, 308.
[18] 2 Peter. 3:9; 1 Tim. 2:4.

Coming to a decision to accept God's offer of salvation begins with an understanding and acknowledgment of one's standing with God. Sin separates humanity from God. Sin is a, "state of alienation from God."[19] Everyone has sinned[20] and deserves eternal separation from God.[21] A person can do nothing in his or her own power to rectify the situation. God solved the problem through the work of His Son, who was born and lived among people yet was without sin.[22] Jesus offered Himself as the sacrifice to meet the demands of sin for those who would take His offer of grace and accept Him as Savior. Parents can be instrumental in showing children their sinfulness while still loving them unconditionally, following the pattern of Jesus by condemning sin but loving sinners.[23]

Once their children have chosen salvation, parents have a special opportunity to nurture spiritual growth through the home and lead their children toward Christ-likeness. When spiritual disciplines are modeled in the home at the family altar, children learn the importance of such habits. As children are taught "the spiritual disciplines, we are giving spiritual instruction to young disciples, people who will grow up to imitate much more of what we do than what we say."[24] The apostle Paul made a great impact on the life of Timothy, but his mother and grandmother modeled a faith Timothy adopted.[25] It cannot be stated enough: Parents' impact on their children remains strong today.

---

19 Elwell, 1103.
20 Rom. 3:23.
21 Rom. 6:23.
22 Heb. 4:15.
23 John 8:3–11.
24 Hess, 14.
25 2 Tim. 1:5; 3:15.

Chapter 5

Parental Influence

As you read to this point, your mind probably began to drift toward the response of your children to family worship: "My kids will never cooperate for us to do this." My experience is that the older one's children, the more fear parents have they will not want to engage in this time together. Parents of teenagers commonly refer to the difficulty of communicating with their teens, concluding the teens do not want to spend time with their parents. The research of Steve Wright and Chris Graves in their book, *ApParent Privilege,* shatters this preconceived notion.

* Ninety-eight percent of students wanted to pray with their parents as often as or more often than they currently did.
* Ninety-seven percent of students wanted to read the Bible as often as or more often than they currently did.
* Only 10 percent reported reading the Bible with their parents very often.
* When asked if they would follow their parents' advice, 41 percent said they would be very likely to and 54 percent somewhat likely. Only 5 percent would not be likely to follow their parents' advice.
* Students were asked to finish the sentence, "I wish my parents would …" Answers included start a family devotion, read the

Bible with me more, pray with me more, take my Christianity seriously.

The influence of parents on their children cannot be overlooked.

* *USA Today Weekend Magazine* polled 272,400 teenagers and found that 70 percent identified their parents as the most important influence in their lives.
* MVParents.com says, "Nearly three out of four parents believe their children's friends and classmates have the most influence … Yet contrary to what parents think, kids say mom and dad have the biggest impact on the choices they make."
* 1,129 middle school students were asked what the greatest influence in their life was, and parents topped the list with 37 percent.
* MTV and the Associated Press asked those between thirteen and twenty-four, "What makes you happy?" Spending time with family was the top answer to that open-ended question.[26]

Notice that the youth minister did not make the top list of influencers. Those interviewed did not say anything about the church. They did not ask for the newest student devotional to read alone. The heart cry of children can be seen in these statistics; they desire to spend time with their parents, practicing spiritual disciplines. This desire is placed by God within each individual, and as Deuteronomy 6 is fulfilled, this desire is met as God intended.

Could it be the reason the relationship between parents and their children, especially teenagers, is strained is due to that fact parents have not met their greatest need, that of spiritual direction found at the family altar? Parents are viewed by their offspring as being the people who regularly let them know where they went wrong. While correction and discipline are essential in the role of parenting, if that is all the

---

26 Steve Wright and Chris Graves. *ApParent Privilege* (Royal Palm Beach, FL: InQuest Ministries, 2008), 18–24.

children receive from their parents, a wedge is driven between the two generations. When parents use their influence to meet the spiritual needs in the life of their children, the relationship is strengthened.

The earlier the family altar is used in children's lives, the more likely it will remain part of the home. I have several friends whose children are now teenagers, and the strength of the relationship between the parents and children is remarkable. A common denominator is that each family practices family worship at the family altar. The children in these families cannot imagine a home without this key ingredient. As a father of young children, I want to set this standard, so they know nothing other than a family that worships together at the family altar, in addition to worshipping together in the corporate setting with other believers.

Our world today needs parents who will use their position and influence to impact the spiritual lives of their children, understanding that establishing this pattern can impact multiple generations, as they raise children who believe worship at the family altar is the norm.

As I trained couples of Hampton First Baptist Church in family worship at the family altar, two couples of teenage children expressed their hesitancy in introducing this concept to their children. One mother commented, "They will think I am crazy." Yet each couple committed to try. The following week, both couples came back with positive reviews from their teenagers. Rather than commenting on their mother's mental capacity as anticipated, this same mother celebrated that her kids recommended a possible book for them to work through in this setting!

Again, the younger your children, the easier it is to begin and continue family worship at the family altar. It can begin with something as simple as reading Bible storybooks to your toddler. If they are like my children, you might only get through half the book before the limit of their attention span is reached. But as you point out the pictures and lift up the flaps, children become interested in the book. As their interest grows, do not be surprised when they bring the book to you with the desire to climb on your lap and have it read to them. Eventually, the entire book will be read, and it will be added to the regular repertoire. The stories from the Word of God will be ingrained in their minds. Parents with young children can use such books as the foundation for their family worship, reading it and then following it with questions and application.

According to Chap Clark,[27] there are two periods of spiritual development. The first is accepting beliefs, and the second is challenging beliefs. The younger parents begin training their children spiritually, the earlier they will accept their beliefs. It is possible, then, that the child will challenge their beliefs at an earlier age, while still under the influence of their parents. This may be greatest reason such alarming numbers of "church kids" leave the church on going to college. They begin to challenge their beliefs on a college campus, away from the security of their parents and the church where they grew up. Amid this personal struggle, they may have no one to turn to for help. Since they are surrounded by a secular culture, they adopt the views of their newfound friends without any regard for the truth they once accepted.

In the first period, Clark notes it is important for parents to be consistent in their faith and to provide experiences that will connect abstract faith to hands-on relationships and service. It is vital that parents move beyond just attending church and practice spiritual discipline with their children. He urges parents to do whatever it takes to build an extended Christ-centered family around their family. The best place for this is through the church, building a network of families supporting each other. As a network is developed, children and teenagers realize their parents are not the only ones that expect them to act godly. Nor is their family the only one that worships together. Today's church has lost much of the community that was essential in the early church. God did not intend for His children to live alone on an island. Rather, He created us for community. While it might not take a village to raise a child, it does take a church!

When children begin to challenge their beliefs in the second stage, parents can encourage personal ownership of their faith, encourage them to ask the hard questions of life, and help them find the answers in the Bible. When death invades their ranks, lead them to the truths of

---

27 Chap Clark, *Disconnected: Parenting Teens in a MySpace World* (Grand Rapids, MI: Baker, 2007), 113–151.

heaven and the promise of eternal life. When they are faced with peer pressure, allow them to learn lessons from Daniel on the importance of holiness and how to stand in the face of opposition. When they rebel from their parents' leadership, remind them of the biblical structure of the home from Paul in Ephesians. As the world deteriorates and teens are disillusioned with what they see, take them back to Genesis, and allow them to discover the continual devastating effects of sin. As parents help their children with these issues and many more through the lens of Scripture, they are forming a solid faith that will not be shaken. All of this can occur in the home.

The key is getting started. One of the least enjoyable tasks found in my life is weeding flower beds. In the early spring, as the flowers begin to bloom, the flower beds begin to be marked with life. It seems like overnight they are overtaken with weeds. I ignore it as long as I can, looking for any excuse to keep from having to tackle this job. When I am no longer able to run from this chore, I assist my wife with this painful responsibility. It may take several hours, but when the job is completed, the flower beds look great. I usually have to admit it was not as difficult as I intended, and anyone who looks will notice the care that has been given to the flower beds. Plus, my wife is happy! Had the weeds been ignored any longer, they would have overtaken the flower bed and killed all the flowers. All I had to do was get started.

Most parents know God calls them to be the spiritual leaders of their children. But they keep putting it off, just as I do about the flower beds. Some may not know how to get started; I address that in the following pages. The longer parents wait to assume the responsibility, the longer the weeds of the world have to grow in the flower beds of their family. We must get started!

The works of George Barna[28] and Steve Wright and Chris Graves[29] revealed a crisis in the families of born-again Christians. While children

---

28 George Barna, *Transforming Children in Spiritual Champions* (Ventura, CA: Regal Books, 2003), 35, 37, 77–80.
29 Wright, 18–24.

desire their parents to spend time with them focused on spiritual matters, parents leave this responsibility to the church. When today's family model is compared to God's plan as described by the doctrine of the family, as well as the role of parents in each child's salvation and sanctification, the need for change is compelling.

Chapter 6

Clearing the Hurdles

At the 2004 Olympic Games in Athens, Liu Xiang became the first man from China to win an Olympic gold medal in track and field, winning the 110-meter hurdles. He backed that up with the 2007 world title. He was—and still is—China's only track-and-field superstar. But he has yet to clear a hurdle in the past two Olympics. An injury eliminated him from the 2008 games, but an accident that many track athletes fear kept him from competing for a medal in 2012; he clipped the hurdle.

Allen Johnson won the gold medal at the 1996 Olympics. He was known to hit many hurdles in a race throughout the course of his career. In one particular race in 2001, he hit nine of the ten hurdles and still ran a time that amazed onlookers. One of the things that made Johnson great is that he is a master of knowing how to hit hurdles without allowing it to slow him down. In that race, he brushed the majority of the hurdles with his hamstring, sliding over them smoothly, causing a slight rustle but not knocking them down.

Parents who lead their families at the family altar will have to clear hurdles with the ease of an Olympian. One often assumes fulfilling something as scriptural as family worship will be easy. But an understanding of spiritual warfare enlightens Christians to the reality Satan will use every tool at his disposal to cause parents to trip over the hurdles.

A common hurdle, and maybe the tallest, is time. Everyone is busy. Families are busy. We live in a fast-paced world and find ourselves rushing from place to place and commitment to commitment. When families are faced with the need for family worship, rarely does a parent ignore the scriptural basis. Still, "I don't have the time," or, "Show me where I can fit it in, and I will do it," are quick responses.

My wife and I understand this hurdle. Jennifer commutes to work, and when she gets home and we eat together, we have fewer than two hours before the kids go to bed. Church commitments take at least two evenings a week and then the kids have dance one night a week. Then there is homework to do, plus ball practice during the appropriate seasons. I know what it is like to trip over the hurdle of time. However, I also admit we are able to find time to watch our favorite television shows. The kids can stay up a little later if we are working on a project or they want to watch the end of a movie. We find time to do what we want to do. I believe that true for all families.

A key to clearing the hurdle of time is prioritizing family worship. Set a regular time, and do not allow anything to interfere with it. As mentioned previously, some families use the time at the dinner table, while others gather before the kids go to bed. When family worship becomes part of the family's routine and has a place of importance, you will find time for it.

Another hurdle is the parents' lack of confidence in leading family worship. Many adults are paralyzed with fear when it comes to praying publicly. Others have watched the grimaces of their peers when they sing, while some do not read aloud very well. Even though they are in the comforts of their own homes and not in public, parents see sets of eyes staring at them and do not believe they can lead family worship. This is probably more indicative of men, who regularly lack the emotional involvement needed within the home for a family to be strong. They are not at ease in their homes, because the relationships with those they attempt to lead are weak. The weaker the relationship, the less likely individuals are to overlook shortcomings.

A key to clearing the hurdle of lack of confidence is to rely on the power of God and His giving you what you need to lead family worship.

While there is no spiritual gift of "family worship leader" listed in Scripture, Christians must understand God equips them to carry out His work. When God blesses individuals with the responsibility of being parents, He equips them to fulfill that role.

When I became a parent, I had no idea what I was supposed to do. We attended a childbirth class, where I expected to get some training on the demands of fatherhood, but it only focused on the birth process. I remember thinking, *What am I going to do?* I had never changed a diaper. When I held children and they got upset, I handed them back to their parents. I was now going to be the parent who received the crying child, and I had no idea how to pacify her. I figured it out by getting involved in parenting responsibilities. The same is true for family worship. Take the responsibility, and start figuring out what it will take in your home, and you do it all through God's power and gifts in your life.

A third common hurdle is the lack of cooperation among children. Parents of teenagers and pre-teens believe their children do not want to participate in family worship, or they fear it will be awkward to begin something new. Research presented in the previous chapter shatters those excuses. Parents with younger children often do not want to battle the "hassle" that might arise from a family gathering and sitting still for a few minutes. In most churches, we ship our children off to the nursery, so we do not have to fight with them to be quiet during church. So why do we want to choose that battle at home?

The key to clearing the hurdle of lack of cooperation is to have a plan. Congregations can tell when their pastor is not prepared. He rambles on and on, telling story after story that do not connect. While he says much, he does not say much of substance. The congregation looks at the clock repeatedly and leaves with its spiritual need of being fed the Word of God unmet. Similarly, when parents just "wing it," children know it and will take advantage of the lack of preparation. Their parents' frustration increases. A plan helps prevent that frustration.

The plan for family worship does not have to be elaborate. Donald Whitney shares three guidelines in his book, *Family Worship: In the*

Bible, in History, and in Your Home.[30] The guidelines are: brevity, regularity, and flexibility.

While some families could gather for a deep, theological discussion, that is not the goal of the average family. The attention span of children may force brevity, leading to a simple time together with a focus on God. While many parents feel inadequate, any parent, regardless of education level, biblical knowledge, or any other measure, can lead family worship. As mentioned earlier, time restraints are a hurdle, so families need to understand family worship can fit in their schedule if they make necessary adjustments. The amount of time at the family altar will differ for each family, depending on the age and maturity of the children, but fifteen to twenty minutes is probably a maximum for even the oldest children.

I have shared this material with parents who eagerly begin to have a family worship time. Only a few months later, they no longer met together as a family. A common mistake is not setting a regular time to gather for family worship. While they committed to a weekly gathering, there was no set time, so it was consistently pushed back on the family schedule until it was no longer included on the family schedule. With regularity, the family will make family worship part of their routine.

While a plan is important, if it is stringent and there is no room for flexibility, the family, especially the leader, can be discouraged by a lack of cooperation. Plans rarely unfold the way they were designed. As the family gathers, it is important everyone understands it is permissible to ask a question or do something different, as long as it applies to the topic. Sing a song or share another story in the Bible that relates. It is not a catastrophe if one of the kids leads in prayer and forgets to mention any of the prayer requests that were discussed. Inflexibility often leaves family worship time marked with frustration, so parents need to understand it is fine if things go differently than planned. The next three chapters will focus on the main elements of family worship.

Many parents find themselves like Moses when they are faced with

---

30 Donald Whitney, *Family Worship: In the Bible, in History, and in Your Home.* Shepherdsville, KY: Center for Biblical Spirituality, 2005.

the responsibility of their children's spiritual development: "Who am I?" Others begin to immediately offer excuses: "What if they do not believe me?" Or, "I am not a good speaker." You might even get to the point of exclaiming, "Send someone else!"

Just as the Lord did not remove His call from Moses' life due to his excuses and plea, parents should not expect the Lord to remove their call as the leader of the children's spiritual development. Moses remained dependent on the Lord in order to lead the people out of Egypt and to the Promised Land. Parents must remain dependent on the Lord if they are going to effectively serve as the spiritual leader of their homes.

The Lord sent Aaron to assist Moses, although throughout Exodus it is apparent Moses increases in the leadership between the two men and Aaron assumes a supporting role. The husband has been given the responsibility of being the spiritual leader of his home, and he has been given a wife to assist him, just as Aaron assisted Moses. It is a reality in today's world—and church—that women are often the spiritual leaders. So if you are a wife and cannot get your husband to lead, consider how you can assist him in increasing his spiritual leadership. The man who said he was not an eloquent speaker later stood before the masses and spoke the Word of God to them. The husband and wife are a team in family worship, assisting each other.

If you are a single parent, you might be alone in this responsibility and feel overwhelmed. It is important to surround yourself with people who can support you. Moses sent Joshua and some of the men to fight the Amalekites in Exodus 17, and as long as Moses held up his hands, the Israelites were winning the battle. When he lowered his hands, the Israelites were defeated. So Aaron and Hur held up his hands until the battle was over, and Israel was victorious.

Single parents need to find someone who can figuratively hold up their hands. It is difficult to lead alone as the frustrations mount. The best place to find people to help is the church, specifically, a small group or Sunday school class. Join other parents leading their families spiritually, and ask them to help you. As Christians, we are in this battle together.

Remember Liu Xiang? After he hit the hurdle in the 2012 Olympics, he lay on the track, clutching his lower right leg. When he got up, he tried to head to the nearest exit but was pointed back to the race area. He managed to make his way the length of the race route the only way he could, using his one good leg. When that slow, awkward trek was complete, another hurdler, Balazs Baji of Hungary, went over and raised Liu's hand in the air, as if to signify he was the winner.

While family worship time may include times of injury due to hitting the hurdle, if you continue to practice this discipline, you are a winner. It is better to limp to the finish than to completely quit during the race.

Chapter 7

The Discipline of Prayer

The spiritual discipline of prayer is essential in family worship, just as it is essential in one's daily life. Richard Foster notes prayer is the most central spiritual discipline because it ushers us into perpetual communion with the Father. To pray is to change. Prayer is the main avenue God uses to transform us.[31]

Prayer is often used at the start of worship services, at the beginning of a meal, and before a big decision, much like the national anthem is used at a ball game; it is a ritual. Prayer, though, is much more than a ritual. It is an encounter, a conversation with the Supreme God.

Many view prayer like the businessman who was late for an important meeting and couldn't find a parking space. As he frantically circled the block, the man got so desperate he decided to pray. Looking toward heaven, he said, "Lord, take pity on me. If you find me a parking space, I'll go to church every Sunday for the rest of my life. And not only that, I'll give up drinking." Miraculously, a parking space appeared. The guy looked up again and said, "Never mind. I found one."

The only way prayer will become something other than a tool to be used in emergencies is by teaching and modeling for our children

---

31 Richard J. Foster, *Celebration of Discipline: The Path to Spiritual Growth* (San Francisco: Harper, 1988), 33.

its importance. Christian families have dropped the ball in this area. A reason the lack of godliness is rampant in today's world is due to prayerlessness. This deficiency can be addressed through the practice of family worship.

The heroes of Christianity valued prayer. Scripture records Jesus going before sunrise to a secluded place and praying (Mark 1:35). A crisis arose in the early church that tempted the apostles to invest their energies in other important tasks. But they determined to focus continually on prayer and the ministry of the Word (Acts 6:4). Martin Luther said, "I have so much business I cannot get on without spending three hours daily in prayer." John Wesley devoted two hours to prayer daily and said, "God does nothing but in answer to prayer." Adoniram Judson took time to withdraw from business activities to pray seven times a day: at dawn, at nine, at twelve, at three, at six, at nine, and at midnight.[32]

Jesus expects us to pray. "And when you pray ..." (Matt. 6:5), "But when you pray ..." (Matt. 6:6), "And when you pray ..." (Matt. 6:7), "This, then, is how you should pray ..." (Matt. 6:9). "So I say to you: Ask ... ; seek ... ; knock ..." (Luke 11:9). "Then Jesus told His disciples ... they should always pray" (Luke 18:1).

The New Testament is clear that we should pray. Colossians 4:2 says, "Devote yourselves to prayer." "When you make something a priority, when you will sacrifice for it, when you will give time to it, you know you are devoted to it. God expects Christians to be devoted to prayer."[33]

Paul tells us to "pray continually" in 1 Thessalonians 5:17. This command reminds Christians that prayer is a relationship. This command has caused many to wonder how they would do anything else if they prayed continually, but Whitney adds clarity by stating, "You might think of praying without ceasing as communicating with God on one line while also taking calls on another."[34]

This expectation is more than a requirement; it is also an invitation.

---

32 Foster, 34.
33 Donald S. Whitney, *Spiritual Disciplines for the Christian Life* (Colorado Springs, CO: NavPress, 1991), 67.
34 Ibid., 68.

Hebrews 4:16 says, "Let us then approach the throne of grace with confidence, so that we may receive mercy and find grace to help us in our time of need." Prayer, then, is also an opportunity to receive the mercy and grace of God.

When I read of people like John Wesley praying two hours a day and Adoniram Judson praying seven times a day, the shortcomings in my prayer life are evident. God used these men, and many others who valued prayer, in great ways to spread the Gospels. A prerequisite for being used by God is being a man or woman of prayer.

Even when you pray before meals and have a regular quiet time, you probably still fall short of praying two hours a day. I do not think God is as concerned with a set amount of time as He is with our dependence on Him. Prayerfulness is a continual reminder of that dependence.

After sharing Adoniram Judson's prayer routine in a public setting, one participant began thinking about that model. He later called me and reported that if he prayed at all three meals, when he got up, when he went to bed, on the way to work, and on the way home from work, that would be seven times! When personal prayer is a priority, we will find the time to pray.

Valerie Hess and Marti Garlett recommend over a period of time, developing a rule of prayer that works for you. What is the best time of day to have a set time for prayer? Where? At home? In the car? At your desk at work? How long will it last? They suggest a simple rule of prayer by saying the Lord's Prayer, as a starting point, three times a day: at nine in the morning, at noon, and at three in the afternoon. The early church used those times. That schedule can be tweaked to pray when you drop the kids off at school, at lunch, and right before the kids come home from school. You could also use your morning commute to work, your lunch break, and your commute home at the end of the workday. Figure out a way to remind yourself to stop and pray.[35]

Hess and Garlett also emphasize the need for "javelin prayers,"

---

35 Valerie E. Hess and Marti Watson Garlett, *Habits of a Child's Heart: Raising Your Kids with the Spiritual Disciplines* (Colorado Springs, CO: NavPress, 2004), 41–43.

quick prayers we say on the run.[36] Examples include, "Jesus, help me remember the answer to this test question," "God, help me to love this unhappy clerk," "Lord, show me how to help this frustrated customer," and "Father, thank you for loving me." It is important to train ourselves to pray continually, whether that is for a set, longer period of time or a quick prayer in a time of need.

I have never met a Christian who did not believe in the importance of prayer. Why, then, do we not pray? Whitney gives five reasons so many believers confess they do not pray as they should[37]:

1. A lack of discipline. Prayer is never planned and gets crowded out by more urgent things. Just as it was mentioned about the lack of planning for family worship, if there are not times planned for personal prayer, it will not occur.

2. People doubt anything will actually happen if they pray. People have prayed for things the Lord chose to answer differently than they anticipated. I see this regularly when people pray for a loved one to be healed, only to see that person pass away. "What's the use?" becomes their attitude about prayer. Jesus, though, taught us to pray persistently, not giving up (Luke 11:5–13; 18:1–5).

3. A lack of sensing the nearness of God. Prayerlessness causes us to be marked by sinfulness, which distances us from God. When we are not near to God, we do not recognize our dependence on Him, so we neglect prayer.

4. When there is little awareness of the need for prayer. Some parts of life are manageable. When life is going good, we can handle it alone. It is in those times that we should thank God for our current state and prepare for the arrival of what we cannot manage on our own.

5. When the awareness of the greatness of God and the gospel is dim. This may be the main reason prayerlessness is prevalent. We forget who God is and what He can do.

---

36 Ibid., 40.
37 Ibid., 69–70.

Christians can allow their failures in prayer to lead to an even lesser desire for prayer. It is vital to remember that "God always meets us where we are and slowly moves us along into deeper things."[38] Christians cannot wait until they feel like praying. "Prayer is like any other work; we may not feel like working, but once we have been at it for a bit, we begin to feel like working … Our prayer muscles need to be limbered up a bit and … we will find that we feel like praying."[39]

The disciples asked Jesus to teach them to pray (Luke 11:1). Parents must also teach their children how to pray. Using Jesus' teachings on prayer in the Sermon on the Mount (Matt. 6:9–15), there are five principles of effective prayer.

Value God as Father
To personally address God as "Father" may not seem out of the ordinary to us today, but it was absolutely revolutionary in Jesus' day. Throughout the Old Testament, there was a distance between humans and God. You can search from Genesis to Malachi, and you will not find one individual speaking of God as Father.

When Jesus addresses God, He always referred to Him as "Father." The word He used was "Abba," a common Aramaic word with which a child would address his or her father. It meant something similar to "daddy" but with a more reverent touch than when we use it. The best rendering is "Dearest Father."

Jesus teaches the disciples to pray by calling God their Father, their Abba. Jesus transferred the Fatherhood of God from a theological doctrine into an intense, practical experience, and He taught His disciples to pray with the same intensity. We can affectionately call God "Abba," or, "Dearest Father," but we do it with a deep sense of wonder and reverence.

When my children were learning to talk, I practiced with them to say, "Daddy." I wanted them to say that long before they said, "Momma." The first time each of them said, "Da-Da," I held a small celebration! I

---

38 Foster, 35.
39 Foster, 45.

love to hear my children call my name. It is my delight to do anything for my children—within reason. Our heavenly Father loves to hear His children call His name, and He delights in answering our prayers.

As we teach our children to pray, we must impress on them the honor and privilege we have to call God "Father." We must also teach them how to respect His holy name.

Desire the Will of God

"Your kingdom come" is a call for God to continue to work. The context of the rest of the prayer leads me to conclude that praying, "Your kingdom come," is focused on bringing men and women into obedient conformity to the Father's will. Those who are in God's kingdom strive to do God's will.

Praying, "Your kingdom come, Your will be done, on earth as it is in heaven," demands a depth of commitment from us. It is an invitation for God to conquer us. It is a plea for God to deliver us from ourselves. Praying these words is a surrender of our desires, dreams, goals, and other personal things, choosing to follow the will of God.

God's will is done in heaven gladly and with no reservation. It is possible to say, "Your will be done," in a tone of bitter resentment, but that is not what God wants. It is His desire that the will of His children matches His will. And when it does not, praying for the will of God asks Him to do what is necessary to make His will prevail in our lives.

Teaching children to desire the will of God accompanies an understanding of surrender. As children grow older, they begin to make plans for their lives. Many want to be doctors, while others want to be on the police force. Lots of boys want to be professional football players, while girls dream of being a princess. Parents usually support these claims in younger children, buying them toy doctor's kits, police uniforms, and letting them play football. Do we ever ask them if they are willing to follow God if He has other plans for their lives? During your family worship time, parents can teach their children about the will of God and surrender by sharing personal stories where God altered their plans. Parents can challenge their children to surrender their goals if God has other plans.

Recognize Your Needs

God wants us to pray for provision. It is the first thing we are to pray for when we pray for ourselves. It is not, though, an invitation to pray for everything in a Christmas wishbook. It is a call to pray for "bread," the physical and spiritual necessities of life. It is an invitation to come to God with requests others might call small. One of the precious realities of our Christian life is that God cares for the simple, ordinary, day-to-day things of life. Jesus taught that even supposedly trivial matters are important to God.

Praying for daily bread fosters a daily dependence on God. Just as the children of Israel had to gather manna each day during their journey out of Egypt, Jesus taught that we are to have a daily dependence on God to meet our needs. We are not just to call out to God when a need arises; rather, we are to make it part of our daily lives, even when we are not aware of a pressing need.

Most Christians effectively practice this principle of prayer. The problem is that it is often the only principle that can be found in our prayers. When our prayers are marked completely by cries of help in times of need, we have an imbalance.

While we regularly have this imbalance, I often see we do not call out to God about our needs until we realize we cannot meet them ourselves. We try to fix the problem in our limited human wisdom, and it is not until the problem grows larger that we call out to God for "bread." As our children share their struggles, we can use our family worship time to pray together for God to provide. A regular part of family worship time should be asking for the prayer requests of your children. They will mention those who are sick and friends who told them something that needs God's help. But they will also share with you about the bully at school, the difficult test coming up, the peer pressure they face, and the many other struggles they face.

A common difficulty with parents, especially parents of teenagers, is communicating effectively with their children. Parents' intuition leads them to know when something is wrong or bothering their children. But when they ask, "What is wrong?" the response is usually, "Nothing." Family worship can increase the communication of a family as each member shares needs and prays for the Lord to provide.

Seeks Forgiveness

We are to ask God to forgive us. This is an easy part of prayer because we all know we sin on a daily basis and need God's forgiveness. When the Holy Spirit convicts us of a sin in our lives, it is imperative we ask God to forgive, to no longer hold that sin against us. We are promised in 1 John 1:9 that if we confess our sins, "He is faithful and just and will cleanse us from all unrighteousness." As a child of God, this fact is a reason for celebration!

Jesus goes further than asking for forgiveness, though, when He says we pray for forgiveness, "as we forgive those who trespass against us." St. Augustine called this request, "the terrible petition," because he realized if we pray it with an unforgiving heart, we are actually asking God *not* to forgive us. Charles Spurgeon said, "Unless you have forgiven others, you read your own death-warrant when you repeat the Lord's Prayer."

No part of Jesus' teaching is clearer, and there are no exceptions to it. He does not say we are supposed to forgive to a certain point. We are to forgive them all, regardless of how spiteful and mean they are, and regardless of how often they are repeated. If we do not, we will not be forgiven of our own sinfulness.

In Matthew 18, Peter asked Jesus how many times a man should forgive someone. Peter was probably the spokesman for the entire group of apostles, and he asked if he should forgive seven times. To Peter and the other apostles, forgiving someone of an offense seven times was more than sufficient. I believe they expected Jesus to commend them for their willingness to forgive an offense so many times. However, Jesus responded they should forgive "seventy times seven." Peter's mind was blown with the thought of forgiving someone 490 times! Jesus' point was that His children live a lifestyle of forgiveness. We are not to carry around a clipboard to keep count of the number of times an individual is forgiven so that if we reach 490, we are done. Rather, Jesus expects us to forgive as we have been forgiven—completely and with no regard to number.

As parents, it is our responsibility to teach our children that their sin is an affront to God. As we teach them to pray, teach them to ask for forgiveness. We also need to teach them to forgive those who have wronged them. Again, your family worship time is a great time to discuss how a family member was wronged and how he or she can respond godly. Parents often know where their children need to offer forgiveness, and it can even be forgiveness toward a parent. So challenge them to forgive as they have been forgiven.

Asks for Spiritual Protection

No one can help being exposed to temptation, and Jesus does not instruct us to pray we will be completely spared from being tempted. The reality is that temptation is good for us, as it is necessary for the development of our moral character.

Temptation molded the life and ministry of Jesus Himself. When He prayed, "Deliver us from the evil one," He personally knew the evil of Satan. At the beginning of His ministry, after being in the wilderness and fasting for forty days, Satan offered Him bread (if He changed the stone to bread), and God offered Him a way to no longer face temptation. Satan wanted Jesus to worship him, but Jesus knew he was the prince of liars and that worship was reserved for God alone. Jesus used Scripture to defeat the temptation.

Jesus faced other temptations in His ministry. He served with hard-headed men who did not understand His complete mission. Plus, He regularly encountered opposition from religious leaders. The temptation would have been great to flee from the cross and the events that led to it, but Jesus personally knew the spiritual protection offered by His Father.

The proper prayer regarding temptation is not that we be delivered from all temptation, for facing and overcoming it are necessary for the health of our souls. But praying for spiritual protection does ask God to deliver us from overpowering temptations, recognizing we are weak and liable to fold. This proper praying forces us to confess we might fall, increasing our dependence on the Lord.

Temptation is real in the lives of our children, and we need to pray together at the family altar for the Lord to deliver each of us.

An effective way to teach your children about prayer is to focus on one of the five principles during family worship. Talk about the principle and model how to pray. Then let the children demonstrate their understanding of the principle. This can be done as the family takes turns stating a need they have and asking the Lord to provide. Individuals can share temptations and have the family pray for them, while someone else might share how he or she needs to forgive someone as the family member has been forgiven. The important part is that the family is praying together. When parents take on this responsibility, they will find prayer becomes an integral part of their children's lives.

Chapter 8

The Discipline of Bible Study

While families today may not gather at the family altar for prayer as often as in generations past, most Christian homes can say prayer occurs in the home because they pray before meals, at bedtime, and maybe at another routine time. However, the discipline of Bible study, in my experience, is practiced less than prayer because we have bought into the idea that Bible study is reserved for the church.

As I mentioned in a previous chapter, I love the church and do not want to sound derogatory. But the church has helped create the shortfall of Bible study in the home because the church does Bible study so well. By definition, Sunday school is the foundational strategy in the local church, and most churches do it well. The best teachers in the church teach Sunday school, and the literature options are plentiful. The teaching time in Sunday school is traditionally longer than the sermon the pastor delivers during the worship service!

Churches that have Wednesday evening services usually have a prayer meeting and Bible study for their adults. The prayer meeting aspect is normally confined to a few minutes of sharing about who is sick and in need of prayer, and then someone prays for them. After the quick prayer time, the pastor or a gifted teacher from the congregation leads the church in Bible study.

Churches also offer Bible studies at other times throughout the week. There are women's studies, men's studies, studies for adults with children, studies for married couples, studies for students; the list goes on. Because we are inundated with Bible studies at church, we neglect this spiritual discipline at home. Parents who fulfill their responsibility toward the spiritual development of their children make the Word of God a fundamental part of their homes.

The apostle Paul instructs followers of Christ: "Do not conform to the pattern of this world, but be transformed by the renewing of your mind" (Rom. 12:2). The mind is renewed by applying it to those things that will transform it. Paul also writes, "Finally, brothers, whatever is true, whatever is noble, whatever is right, whatever is pure, whatever is lovely, whatever is admirable—if anything is excellent or praiseworthy—think about such things" (Phil. 4:8). Bible study is the primary vehicle to bring us to "think about such things."[40]

Foster defines Bible study as a "specific kind of experience in which through careful attention to reality, the mind is enabled to move in a certain direction."[41] This definition points out that the end goal of Bible study is not information but transformation. A problem with many Bible studies is that the focus is only on information, on giving all the details. While that information is important, the study of the Bible should lead to action. Our minds should be renewed. Our hearts should be purified. Our actions should be challenged. James gives the command to not just hear the Word but do what it says (James 1:22).

The need for parents to teach God's Word to their children is seen in Deuteronomy 11:18–21. Amid a challenge from God to keep His Word and its commands, the original audience is reminded their children did not see the acts of God that led to the deliverance of Israel from bondage in Egypt. It was the responsibility of the parents to teach God's Word and His ways to their children. "The purpose of this instruction is to direct the mind repeatedly and regularly toward certain modes of thought about God and human relationships."[42]

---

40 Richard J. Foster, *Celebration of Discipline: The Path to Spiritual Growth* (San Francisco: Harper, 1988), 62.

41 Ibid., 63.

42 Ibid., 64.

This passage shows that the parents were to make God's Word prominent in their homes (verses 18, 20). God is saying, "In everything you do, make sure to saturate your children with my words. Write them on the doorframes and on the walls so that every place they turn they will encounter them. Impart the truth of God to your children."

The passage also instructs parents to take advantage of every opportunity (verse 19). God did not intend for the parents to teach their children His Word only at home. He intended that as the family lived life together—everywhere they went and everything they did—they were to teach the Word. This has never been more important in the fast-paced society in which we live today. Families are constantly going from one event to the next, with very little time at home.

Moses points out children would benefit from their parents' faithfulness in teaching (verse 21). Deuteronomy 11 is a chapter full of if-then statements, where Moses points out if the people of Israel follow His commands, He will bless them by allowing them to take possession of the Promised Land. Verse 21 states the result of parents teaching the ways of God is, "Your days and the days of your children may be many in the land."

The Israelites did not have a book they could read to their children. Verbal instruction ensured another generation heard about the deliverance the Lord provided and the expectations He set. The Bible remains the top-selling book in the world today, but parents cannot fulfill their spiritual responsibility to educate their child by simply buying them a Bible. It is imperative they teach God's Word to their children. We are always one generation away from God's story no longer being told.

In my first pastorate, I coached a summer baseball team comprised of children ages eight to ten for three years. The team was sponsored by the school and played teams from similarly sized communities in a three-county area. I am almost certain I had this opportunity because no one else wanted it! My first team was the best of the three I had; we finished second in the standings during the regular season. The first-place team beat us both times we played, and no one had gotten close to beating them. They had a set of twin brothers who carried the team and were some of the best athletes I have ever seen at that age. At the end of the year, we met again in the finals of the league tournament. I could tell my team was afraid of this team and the two brothers, one of whom was pitching.

As we waited for the game to start, I decided I was going to give a pep talk. I had not done this all year, but I just knew it was going to work to motivate my kids and lead to a victory. "Boys," I started, "playing this team reminds me of the time David fought Goliath." I was ready to give his talk with all the great delivery of a sermon—until I heard one say, "Who?"

I asked around and no one had ever heard of David and Goliath! These kids were being raised in the heart of the Bible belt, in a community with a population of six hundred that had seven churches, yet they did not know about David and Goliath. Not all the kids had the privilege to grow up in church. Being able to reach these families was one of the reasons I agreed to coach the team. At least half the team did attend church, several of them attended the church where I was pastor, yet none of them knew a story I thought all of us knew.

After I told the story of David and Goliath and made the connections to the situation we were facing as a team, one of the kids asked, "Is that a true story?"

That situation opened my eyes to the reality that the Word of God is not being taught in our homes. It is not being taught in the homes of professing Christians, and sadly, it is not being taught in many churches. It is a reality that broke my heart as an early twenty-something, and one I continue to see regularly. Even the "church kids" do not know God's Word because Mom and Dad have not impressed it on them.

For those of you wondering, we did not win the game. My pep talk did not work to motivate us to victory. But the experience I had that one day led me to the commitment to equip parents to teach God's Word in their homes. All those boys from that team are now either college students or in the workforce. They will be starting families soon. For many of them, they will not have the Word to pass to their children, because it was never given to them.

As parents lead their family worship time, effective Bible study goes beyond hearing a lesson and answering some discussion questions.

It takes effort. Parents should lead their family to meditate on the text. Meditation has been misidentified due to the coming of new age philosophy as something you do when you cross your arms and legs, close your eyes, and make a humming sound in a dark room. However, meditation is defined as, "deep thinking on the truths and spiritual realities revealed in Scripture for the purposes of understanding, application, and prayer."[43]

When individuals or families read a text from Scripture and do not meditate on the text, they have only done half of what was needed for spiritual vitality. I read through the Bible each year, but one thing I can find myself doing is checking off the day's readings without meditating on what I read. This trap leads me to a ritual that does nothing to change my life, which was a characteristic of the Pharisees that Jesus regularly attacked.

Parents can also fall into this trap when they read the Bible with their kids but do not apply it to their lives. The Bible, then, becomes nothing more than a bedtime storybook. One does not have to be a trained theologian to answer the questions, "What is the text saying?" and, "What does it mean to me?" Answering those questions causes one to meditate on the text.

There is a specific scriptural connection between success, in God's eyes, and the practice of meditation on God's Word found in Joshua 1:8. God's words to Joshua as the leader of God's people were: "Do not let this Book of the Law depart from your mouth; meditate on it day and night, so that you may be careful to do everything written in it. Then you will be prosperous and successful." These words come from the commissioning of Joshua to lead Israel to the Promised Land, and the key to success was not military strength, tactical intelligence, or any other thing of humankind. If Joshua was going to be a successful leader, he must meditate on the Word of God. I believe there is a strong correlation between the demise of many families and the lack of meditation. Success is not guaranteed without meditation.

---

43 Donald S. Whitney, *Spiritual Disciplines for the Christian Life* (Colorado Springs, CO: NavPress, 1991), 48.

"True success is promised to those who meditate on God's Word, who think deeply on Scripture, not just at one time each day, but at moments throughout the day and night. They meditate so much that Scripture saturates their conversation. The fruit of their meditation is action. They do what they find written in God's Word and as a result God prospers their way and grants success to them."[44]

Psalm 1:1–3 also contains promises regarding meditation. The psalmist calls those who meditate on the Word of God "blessed." Whitney notes that "when we delight in God's Word we think about it, that is, we meditate on it, at times all throughout the day and night. The result of such meditation is stability, fruitfulness, perseverance, and prosperity."[45]

Scripture memorization is another discipline of Bible study that can be practiced in the context of the family. It, too, has been neglected. The common excuse for not memorizing Scripture is the difficulty, or impossibility, of remembering. I have noticed, though, that those who regularly use that reasoning have no problem remembering the lyrics to their favorite songs! They can remember multiple Internet passwords and personal identification numbers, but they cannot remember the location to a passage of Scripture. I have concluded that we are just too lazy to give the effort it takes to memorize Scripture.

I remember being at a youth conference about fifteen years ago, where the speaker stressed the need for Scripture memorization. He had everyone stand up, including the adults, and asked them to think of how many verses of Scripture they knew, other than John 3:16. "If you know less than five verses, sit down," he started. Over half of the approximately one thousand in attendance sat down. He continued in increments of five, and by the time he got to twenty, no one was standing. There were youth ministers and other youth leaders in this crowd, but no one in attendance had memorized more than twenty verses of Scripture.

---

44 Ibid.
45 Ibid., 49.

Donald Whitney lists five benefits of Scripture memorization: [46]

1. Supplies spiritual power. When Satan tempted Jesus in the desert, Jesus defeated every temptation by using Scripture. Matthew 4 records that each time Satan tempted, Jesus responded, "It is written," followed by a quotation of Scripture.

   In Paul's description of the armor of God in Ephesians 6, he calls the Word of God, "the Sword of the Spirit," the only offensive weapon found in the armor. By refusing to memorize Scripture, we deny ourselves the power available through the Lord.

2. Strengthens your faith. Scripture is full of promises and reminders of how God works. When the world is against us and it feels like all of life is falling apart, when we can recall Scripture that has been memorized, we receive encouragement and our faith is strengthened.

3. Helps in witnessing and counseling. It is alarming that the average church member never shares their faith. Plus, they do not know how to respond when an acquaintance comes to them with a spiritual need. When we memorize Scripture, we have the tools needed to lead people to Christ and offer practical support to those in need.

4. Is a means of God's guidance. God will never lead anyone in a way that contradicts His Word. How often do we search for God's will without any knowledge of His Word? When we store His Word in our hearts through memorization, we have the guidance we need to live as He intended and make decisions in accordance with His Word.

5. Stimulates meditation. Memorizing the Word of God allows us to continually think about it.

When Addison, our oldest child, was about three years old, Jennifer and I began to help her learn a weekly Bible verse. I was surprised how easy she learned them. She is now seven and is learning passages of four

---

[46] Ibid., 42–44.

to five verses. We each have used many excuses for our lack of Scripture memorization, but we were challenged by our child's eagerness and ability to memorize one verse a week. As Jennifer and I help her learn these verses, we are also learning (or refreshing) them. That is why I believe the family is a great place for Scripture memorization. It engages multiple generations in storing the Word of God in their hearts.

While teaching first-aid clinics on a mission trip to Chile in October 2010, Bible stories were shared between first-aid topics. We were in a one-room school that comfortably seated its twenty children in their desks, but we crammed over fifty adults in this little room. Throughout the first-aid topics, the audience talked among themselves and moved around. However, when the presenter stated, "I would like to share a story with you from the Bible," all those in attendance got quiet, sat up, and focused on the presenter. After the day, a group of three men approached one of the missionaries and asked if he would return and teach more Scripture because they needed to hear what God had to say. All Christians should have such a hunger for God's Word, but as Donald Whitney points out, "great numbers of professing Christians know little more about the Bible than Third-World Christians who possess not even a shred of Scripture."[47] God intends for it to be taught, meditated upon, and memorized in our homes.

---

[47] Ibid., 28.

Chapter 9

The Discipline of Praise

The three common elements to family worship, developed by Donald Whitney, are pray, read, and sing.[48] The two previous chapters have examined prayer and Bible study, but I prefer the use of "praise" over "sing." Whitney focuses on the expression of praise through song. My focus is on two spiritual disciplines I use to define praise: worship and celebration.

The main reason I focus on praise rather than singing is because most men do not like to sing, especially in a small group. One of my greatest frustrations as a pastor is to look out into the congregation and see men standing, arms folded and eyes roaming during congregational singing. Much has been discussed about this dilemma without anyone coming to a definite reason, other than a conclusion that singing about the love of God and declaring our love for Him reduces one's masculinity. I do not buy into this notion, because I believe God created us all with a desire to worship, and we will worship something or someone.

The man who will not sing at church will not sing at home. Therefore, when we expect a father to lead his family in worship through praying, reading the Bible, and singing, Dad often fails to take the necessary

---

48 Donald S. Whitney, *Family Worship: In the Bible, in History, and in Your Home* (Shepherdsville, KY: Center for Biblical Spirituality, 2005), 17.

leadership because he does not want to sing. A problem of which I am constantly reminded is that dads who do not sing produce sons who do not sing. I see it weekly, where a teenage son stands beside his dad with his arms folded and eyes roaming, just like his father. This cycle can be broken through the use of praise at the family altar.

Fathers should not get all of the blame, though, because both Mom and Dad quit singing with their children as the children age. All parents sing peaceful songs to their infants, hoping to calm them down to allow everyone to get some sleep. As a child matures into a toddler, parents teach songs and the accompanying motions, often acting goofy in the process. Somewhere in the late-toddler years, parents will sing, and their children will respond, "Don't sing!" This directive is normally interpreted that the children do not like the parents' voices, but it probably has more to do with the child's independence and desire to sing alone.

Praise has been reduced to something that happens in a worship service, once or twice a week. A strong personal conviction I hold is that God deserves more than one to two hours a week! Praise should be a daily part of our personal lives, as well as a regular part in the collective life of a family. The family altar is the ideal place for this to occur.

I define praise simply as giving God what He deserves. Praise involves focusing on and responding to God. Praise is observed throughout Scripture. In John 20:28, when the resurrected Jesus appears to Thomas and shows him the scars in His hands and side, praise is what happens when Thomas says to Him, "My Lord and my God!" In Revelation 4:8, we are told that four creatures around the throne praise God day and night without ceasing with, "Holy, holy, holy is the Lord God Almighty, who was, and is, and is to come." Then in verse 11, the twenty-four elders around the throne of God in heaven are said to praise Him by casting their crowns at His feet, falling down before Him, and saying, "You are worthy, our Lord and God, to receive glory and honor and power, for you created all things, and by your will they were created and have their being." In the next chapter, thousands of angels, elders, and living creatures around the heavenly throne of Jesus cry out with a loud voice in praise, "Worthy is the Lamb, who was slain, to receive power and wealth and wisdom and strength and honor and glory and praise" (Rev. 5:12). Immediately following comes praise from every created thing: "To Him who sits on the throne and to the Lamb be praise and honor and glory and power, forever and ever!" (Rev. 5:13).

The Psalms are full of praise with commands to sing, shout, rejoice, and adore. The Old Testament required the sacrifice of bulls and goats, while the New Testament requires the sacrifice of praise. Peter instructs God's people to "declare the praises of Him who called you out of darkness and into His wonderful light" (1 Peter 2:9).

Praise can be viewed as one's response to the person and character of God, while celebration is the response to the work of God. When the family spends time in prayer and sees God answer their prayers, they should be moved to celebrate. When the family studies God's Word and sees how God worked in Scripture and how He still works today in their lives, their response should be to praise.

There are times when Christians allow their feelings and circumstances to hinder their praise. As a pastor, I have encountered people who have no desire to worship corporately in a church setting because of a tragedy in their lives or a time of difficulty, as if God stopped being God during those times and is not worthy of praise. Even when we cannot celebrate how God has worked, we can still worship due to the fact that God did not change. Scripture records Peter and John leaving the Sanhedrin with bleeding backs and praising lips (Acts 5:41). Paul and Silas filled the Philippian jail with songs of praise (Acts 16:25). We cannot allow our circumstances to direct our willingness to praise.

When children celebrate something, they make lots of noise. In family worship, when we encounter the Lord through prayer and Bible study, the outflow of that may be to praise Him through celebration. It is important to keep a list of the prayers God has answered, as well as refresh the mind of the stories of God's provision for His people. "Celebration brings joy into life, and joy makes us strong. Scripture tells us that the joy of the Lord is our strength (Neh. 8:10). We cannot continue long in anything without it."[49]

---

49 Ibid., 191.

Family worship does not replace the corporate worship setting. Believers are expected to participate regularly in corporate worship. Hebrews 10:25 clearly instructs, "Let us not give up meeting together, as some are in the habit of doing. Christianity is not an isolationist religion."[50] Christians are to gather with other believers for the purpose of expressing worship and celebration to God.

Sadly, many Christians have replaced the family worship setting with the corporate setting. The only time they gather for praise is at church. Praise is missing from their homes. Foster states, "Many things can happen in smaller gatherings that, just by sheer size, cannot happen in the larger experience. All of these little experiences of worship will empower and impact the larger Sunday gatherings."[51] When considering corporate praise and personal praise, it is not either/or; rather, it is both/and. Each element enhances the other. When personal praise is practiced, the Sunday gathering is anticipated. The family can use the Sunday experience to further explore the sermon throughout the week, or they might continue to sing a new song that was unveiled during the Sunday worship. Corporate and family worship times are intended to complement each other.

A. W. Tozer said, "If you will not worship God seven days a week, you do not worship Him on one day a week."[52]

---

50 Whitney, *Spiritual*, 92.
51 Foster, 171.
52 Whitney, *Spiritual*, 95.

Chapter 10

Other Family Worship Disciplines

A problem I see in most churches today is that people are more eager to gather for worship than they are to support the ministries of the church. I have been reminded through my ministry of the adage that 80 percent of the work of the church is performed by 20 percent of the people, and 80 percent of the offerings received are given by 20 percent of the people. The plethora of Bible studies and worship services have not impacted this disproportionate ratio. The only thing that will bring about a change is people committing to support the work of the church.

While the importance of prayer, Bible study, and praise at the family altar are not to be reduced, if those are the only spiritual disciplines we model for our children, we will likely raise children who do nothing but attend church as adults. A friend once used the term "spiritual constipation" to describe this condition, noting that many Christians regularly focus on intake, but the intake never produces. As mentioned previously, the church has specialized in offering many Bible studies, yet church leaders face an increasing frustration about a lack of service from those who attend faithfully.

I believe that in order for the 80/20 gap to be reduced, parents must model for their children at least two other spiritual disciplines: service and stewardship. These disciplines take the family altar outside the home, rejoicing in the fact God is not limited to a certain location, but He equips His people for good works. As a parent, it is my desire to raise children who do not know any other way of life than one that serves the Lord in and through the local church, storing up "treasures in Heaven" (Matthew 6:20).

The towel has been called the sign of service.[53] In John 13, Jesus teaches the disciples the importance of serving by washing their feet. Jesus and His disciples gathered to celebrate the Passover and eat what would be their last meal together before Jesus endured the cross. It was customary for the host to provide a servant to wash the guests' feet. As the disciples entered the room, they would have noticed this important part missing from their gathering. This was a lowly task disciples knew had to be performed, yet none of them volunteered to fulfill the obligation. As they reclined at the table, Jesus rose from His place, wrapped a towel around His waist, and washed their feet. Then He commanded each follower to serve as they had been served: "Now that I, your Lord and Teacher, have washed your feet, you also should wash one another's feet. I have set you an example that you should do as I have done for you. Very truly I tell you, no servant is greater than his master, nor is a messenger greater than the one who sent him. Now that you know these things, you will be blessed if you do them" (John 13:14–17).

Today's culture is enveloped in a "me first" attitude that has invaded the church. The reason many people do not serve is because they are so focused on their own concerns that they do not see the needs of others or the needs of the church. Attending a local church has become no different than attending a sporting event. People come and watch the proceedings but never get involved. Parents can begin changing this reality by teaching and modeling their children to serve.

Whitney notes six motives the Bible mentions for serving: obedience; gratitude; gladness; forgiveness, not guilt; humility; love.[54] Notice that guilt, one of the main motivations used to motivate people to complete a task, is missing from this list because it is not a biblical motive. These

---

53 Richard J. Foster, *Celebration of Discipline: The Path to Spiritual Growth* (San Francisco: Harper, 1988), 126.
54 Donald S. Whitney, *Spiritual,* 118–122.

motives come from recognizing what God has done in an individual's life. When we understand the work of God, we know we are to be involved in His work.

I will be forever grateful to Dr. Ken Gore, chair of the Department of Christian Ministries at Williams Baptist College, for assigning his supervised ministry class the Bible study *Jesus on Leadership*. Supervised ministry is the final class for all students in the department, and it was during this class that I was called to my first pastorate. Prior to this call, though, I completed *Jesus on Leadership*, and it changed the way I ministered and has probably kept me from being fired. *Jesus on Leadership* focused on the servanthood of Jesus, most notably, the taking of the towel and washing of the disciples' feet. I was a student athletic trainer in high school and college and had wrapped many ankles during that time, so I knew that feet were nasty! Yet Jesus calls us to such service, meeting the needs around us, regardless of the level of attraction.

Prior to completing *Jesus on Leadership*, I allowed my type A personality to drive my ministry. I believed I would lead by telling people what to do, and I was ignorant enough to think they would respond to my "leadership." It worked in youth ministry because teenagers were accustomed to being told what to do. But I realize now that without this revelation about servant leadership, I would have never survived ministry. God's children are called to serve. If parents do not model and teach this to their children, we will continue to produce generations that focus on their own needs and neglect those of others. While not all our children will be ministers, some will be deacons, others will be Sunday school teachers, and still others will faithfully serve behind the scenes without any title or recognition. Parents can impact future generations and the health of the church by including the discipline of service in their family worship.

This discipline can be instituted in your family by finding a need within the church or community and meeting that need. It may be an older person who needs assistance with yard work or may just want some company. It may be a project at the church that your kids can be involved in at some level. Two examples jump out at me that recently happened in the church I pastor. The first occurred during a countywide canvass we were doing, where we attempted to reach each home in the county to distribute a smoke detector battery, as well as information about how to "fireproof" their life through a relationship with Jesus. As we gathered, one couple had their four-year-old daughter with them, and she was adamant she could help. This girl made every step her dad's team made, walking up to doors (under the watchful eye of her dad) and leaving the information. One of the oldest men in the church was on the team, and he still talks about that day and the work of that little girl—all because one family served together.

The second example took place during a churchwide workday, one of the things church members like to ignore! We were expanding the playground for our children's ministry, and it required putting up more fence. This involves the dreaded tasks of digging postholes and mixing concrete. I challenged the men in the church with young children to participate because, "It is for our kids." Several men gathered that morning, but one father also brought his two teenagers, a boy and a girl, and they worked harder than any of the men. When I thought about the work, there were several other men who left their children at home that Saturday morning. I am sure the two who helped would have rather been at home, but this father modeled for his children the importance of serving. As I watch these two teenagers grow spiritually, I am convinced they will be strong leaders in their church as adults, and they will lead through serving.

Families can also attend mission trips together to further practice service. The past several years have led to an increase in the number of churches of all sizes taking short-term mission trips. Churches with strong youth ministries usually take a youth mission trip in the summer or during spring break, but more churches are starting to offer family mission trips. While youth mission trips are great, there is something about Mom and Dad going on a mission trip with you rather than simply dropping you off at the church and reminding you to behave before driving away. For years, youth ministers have shared stories about their group growing closer due to a mission trip and how the teenagers were challenged in their walk with Christ. Families that serve together on mission trips—whether it is locally, nationally, or internationally—will also find they will grow closer as a family and to the Lord.

The second additional discipline I find key to family worship is stewardship. Stewardship is talked about very little at church and even less in the home because it is regularly equated with money. Pastors do not like to talk about it out of the fear that it appears they are only focused on the money. Church members prefer not to hear messages about stewardship because of their idolatry of money. Stewardship involves much more than money; it is how we manage *everything* the Lord has given us. While this includes financial resources, it also places a focus on how we manage our time, families, spiritual gifts, and every other thing with which we have been blessed.

Jesus tells a story that focuses on stewardship in Matthew 25:14–30. A man was going on a trip, so he called his servants together and divided his wealth among them. One man was given five talents, another two talents, and the final man was given one talent. When the master returned, he found the first two men invested their talents and doubled what they had been given, while the third man buried this talent and only presented what he had been given. The third man was referred to as "wicked," "lazy," and "worthless."

This story teaches us at least six stewardship lessons we need to teach our children.

1. What we have is not ours. There was no doubt in the minds of these servants that the property and money still belonged to the master. They were the possessors but not the owners. Their job was to manage what they were given. Likewise, we must remember everything we have has been given to us and is not really ours anyway. "The earth is the Lord's, and everything in it, the world, and all who live in it" (Psalm 24:1).

2. We are given what we can handle. Notice that each servant receives talents, "according to his ability." Your responsibility is tied to your ability. God's kingdom does not operate according to what is fair but according to what is best.

3. We must invest what we have been given. Even though we do not read any instructions from the master to the servants, two of the three invested and received praise: "Well done, good and faithful servant." These two men understand they were not to simply keep what had been given but were to invest it and present a return.

4. A day of accountability is coming. These men knew the master would return, although it turned out to be a "long time." They knew he would ask them about the possession entrusted to them. We need to understand that Jesus is coming again and will bring a day of reckoning. When we believe this, we are focused on making an eternal return on our investments.

5. What we do with what we have reveals our view of God. The first two men were excited to show their master what they had done, while the third man looked at him as someone who was hard and harsh rather than loving and gracious. When we see God for who He is, we will want to be faithful, and we will focus on properly managing our resources for kingdom purposes.

6. We must use what we have or lose it. The first two servants had their resources increased after they had proven themselves faithful. But the third one lost what he had not used. Christians are called to develop, compound, and multiply what we have been given.

The basic teaching of stewardship to our children is that of the tithe, of giving 10 percent of our income. Some state the tithe was an Old Testament concept and no longer applies to today, since we are not under the Law. But we cannot ignore the fact that Abraham brought a tithe to Melchizedek before the Law was given. Giving of the tithe declares our dependence on the Lord to enable us to live on the remaining 90 percent of our income. It is an acknowledgment of His lordship in our lives. Children need to see this modeled by their parents. I can remember as a child, when I knew things were tight, I would see my parents tithe faithfully. I knew the money could be used for something else, but they modeled for me the need of giving God what was rightfully His.

Parents can also teach stewardship by giving their children an allowance and pointing out the need to tithe from it. It is the same thing with money received for birthdays, Christmas, and any jobs they hold. My wife worked as a lifeguard in the summer at the city pool when she was in high school. One particular Sunday, she wrote a check for her tithe and submitted it during Sunday school. Before church was out that day, the Sunday school director took her check to her dad and asked why she was giving. He could not understand why a teenager would give. But I know why. Her parents taught and modeled the practice, and she knew no other way.

Parents should also consider how they model stewardship in relation to their other possessions. Time is one such area. It is the equalizer of all, since we have the same amount of time in a day. "I don't have time," is probably the number one excuse given each day. The truth is, we have the time but do not manage it properly. Our children see us make sacrifices in order to have the time to do what we want. They also see we do not hold the same priority when it comes to making time to serve through the church or as a family to meet a need.

It is a common occurrence to see parents adjust their schedules and sacrifice to attend their children's sporting events, to take them on a shopping trip, to take them hunting or fishing, or one of many other extracurricular activities. It is just as common to hear these parents say they do not have time to attend church. Or maybe they attend church regularly, but they do not have the time needed to practice family worship disciplines.

Our children need to see us using our spiritual gifts, modeling and teaching that you use the talents God has given to advance His kingdom. They need to see us open our homes to encourage the new family that just moved in the neighborhood, teaching the children God has blessed the family with a home that can be used to bless others. Everything you have is to be managed properly. Your children are watching!

Service and stewardship make family worship a lifestyle and not just a set time when the family gathers. While prayer, Bible study, and praise can be used at any time, service and stewardship are visible expressions of worship.

Chapter 11

Start!

While reading through 1 and 2 Kings, the need for parents to lead their families in family worship disciplines was reinforced. The Israelites' faith was often strengthened or weakened due to the faith of their king. One king who led them away from the Lord was Jeroboam. Jeroboam had an interesting rise to power, as he managed the laborers Solomon used for his huge building projects. One day as Jeroboam went out of Jerusalem, the prophet Ahijah met him on the road and confronted him by tearing his own garment into twelve pieces. He gave ten of them to Jeroboam. This action proclaimed that Jeroboam would become king over ten of the twelve tribes. You can read about all of this starting in 1 Kings 11. Jeroboam became the first king of the Northern Kingdom.

In what Jeroboam considered a good political move, he proposed an alternative form of worship that was idolatrous. He was afraid the people might return to the other two tribes if they continued to journey to Jerusalem for the festivals and observances at the temple. So Jeroboam made two calves of gold that bore a close resemblance to the Canaanite pagan god Baal. This decision diverted people from worshipping at Jerusalem, God's chosen place.

Once this sinful choice was made, Jeroboam's spiritual progress went downhill. He instituted new worship practices at his temples, intentionally making Israelite worship different from that in Jerusalem, though claiming to worship the same God. He appointed priests from tribes other than Levi, and he made several other decisions that polluted worship.

The Lord confronted Jeroboam by sending him an unnamed prophet, who predicted God's judgment on the king and the nation. Although outwardly he appeared to be repentant, Jeroboam would not change his disastrous idolatry. His rebellious, arrogant attitude set the pattern for rulers of Israel for generations to come. Eighteen kings sat on the throne of Israel after his death, but not one of them gave up his pagan worship. It is said of each of these kings, "He did evil in the eyes of the Lord, following the ways of Jeroboam" (1 Kings 15).

As I read this description of each king, I was reminded of the influence a person has on multiple generations. This is why such things as alcoholism are often a multigeneration issue, as is divorce, abuse, and a whole list of other sins. To stop this negative cycle, someone has to step up and declare, "This stops with me."

On the flip side, there were some godly kings in the Southern Kingdom who passed that influence to their sons, who succeeded him. Scripture says things like, "He did right in the eyes of the Lord, just as his father had done."

Parents, we need to understand our importance in the spiritual development of our children. It is my prayer that as you have read this book, you have been convicted of this need and encouraged to take responsibility. Will it be easy? Probably not. Will the hard work be worth it? I believe it will as we create a foundation for our children to do, "right in the eyes of the Lord."

There will be times when you are ready to throw in the towel, but continue leading your children, longing to hear those words, "Well done, good and faithful servant!" God may have only trusted you with a few things, but He has given you a few things of great value to Him—your children. Invest well!

Appendix 1
Weekly Devotionals

The following fifty-two weekly devotionals are intended for parents to read as a launching point for weekly family worship time. The focus of the devotionals are Jesus' words on the Sermon on the Mount, select passages from Ephesians, as well as select Old Testament heroes.

Parents with older children and teenagers may find the entire devotional is appropriate for their children, while the illustrations and some explanation may be more-detailed or too advanced for younger children, especially preschool. In that case, a story Bible is recommended to use, laying a strong foundation for your children. The *Jesus Storybook Bible* by Sally Lloyd-Jones is one such resource that has come highly recommended to me.

Remember: pray, read, and praise. These devotionals will lay out the reading aspect, but you must apply it to your family by asking, "What does this mean to us?" and lead in the prayer and praise.

Week 1
Today, I praise God for: _____

Read Matthew 5:3 and Revelation 3:17–18.

Mickey Cohen was the most flamboyant criminal of the 1950s. At the height of his career, he was persuaded to attend an evangelistic service at which he showed a surprising interest in Christianity. Some prominent Christian leaders began visiting him in an effort to help him accept Christ.

Late one night, after repeatedly being encouraged to accept Christ, Cohen prayed to do so. Hopes ran high among his believing acquaintances, but with the passing of time, no one could detect any change in Cohen's life. Finally, they confronted him with the reality that being a Christian meant he had to give up his friends and change his profession. Cohen balked at that notion: "There are Christian football players, Christian cowboys, Christian politicians; why not a Christian gangster?"

Though many apparently have accepted Christ, they continue to live as they always have. There is no repentance. They remain self-sufficient. They are nowhere near the kingdom, because they have not experienced the poverty of spirit that the first beatitude insists is the initial ground of the kingdom of heaven. We never outgrow this first beatitude.

The word "poor" in Greek denotes a poverty that is so deep, so extreme that the person must obtain his living by begging. He is fully dependent on the giving of others. He cannot survive without help from the outside; he is "beggarly poor." "Blessed are those who are so desperately poor in their spiritual resources that they admit they must have help from outside sources."

If we outgrow this beatitude, we have outgrown our Christianity. That is what was happening in the Laodicean church, which brought the stern words of Revelation 3:17–18. As we are continually aware of our spiritual insufficiency, we are able to continually receive spiritual riches, most notably a closer walk with Christ.

As you pray, admit that you have nothing to commend yourself to God other than the work of Jesus.

Week 2

Today, I praise God for: _____

Read Matthew 5:4 and Romans 3:10–17.

"Blessed are those who mourn" does not mean, "blessed are grim, cheerless Christians," or, "blessed are those who mourn over the difficulties of life." The mourning Jesus refers to is the sorrow that comes from one's spiritual bankruptcy. This is not "feeling badly" about sin, but it is calling "sin," sin and realizing its effects on your life. You are beggarly poor.

It is time to realize our sinful state for what it is apart from God's grace and begin to mourn over its devastating dimensions in our souls, words, and deeds as described in Romans 3: souls (10–12), words (13–14), and deeds (15–17). We must quit rationalizing our sins and call them what they are. The verb form is continuous; we should continually mourn over our sin.

In the early 1980s, Congressmen Daniel Crane and Gerald Studds were censured by the House of Representatives, Crane for having sexual relations with a seventeen-year-old female page and Studds for having relations with a seventeen-year-old male page. Crane admitted tearfully to his district and then to the full House that he, "broke the laws of God and man." He cast a vote in favor of his own censure and faced the Speaker as he announced the tally. Studds, in contrast, acknowledged he was gay in a dramatic speech to the House and defended his relationship with the page as "mutual and voluntary." He noted he had abided by the age of consent and said the relationship did not warrant the "attention or action" of the House. He voted "present" on his censure and heard his verdict from the Speaker with his back to the House.

The saddest thing in life is not a sorrowing heart but a heart that is incapable of grieving over sin, for it is without grace. Without poverty of spirit, no one enters the kingdom of God. Likewise, without its emotional counterpart—grief over sin—no one receives comfort.

As you pray, what sins have you rationalized or excused that you need to mourn?

Week 3

Today, I praise God for: _____

Read Matthew 5:8, James 4:8, and Psalm 86:11–13.

Jesus got worked up over some of the people of His day because they spent an awful lot of time on their outsides: looking good, wearing the right clothes, having long prayer beads dangling down to their knees, their hair all fixed up nice, all washed up, teeth nice and white. They loved to stand in the prominent places in the community and pray aloud. It was a nice show. But that's all it was! Jesus saw through all the pretty and the pretense to what was in their hearts. Using the words of Isaiah, he said, "These people honor me with their lips, but their hearts are far from me." By the way, Jesus was talking about "church folks." Jesus said on another occasion these folks were like whitewashed tombs—all pretty, clean, and white on the outside, but on the inside they were rotting corpses.

"Pure" refers to a clean mind or clean emotions. It can also mean "unmixed, as having no double allegiance." As Jesus is using it here, He refers to a heart that does not bring mixed motives and divided loyalties to its relationship with God. It is a heart of singleness in devotion to God—pure, unmixed devotion.

Pure is then represented by the word "focus," concentration, sincerity, and singleness. Focusing on God with a singleness of heart is one of the biggest challenges to 21st-century Christians. Very few in this crazy age are capable of the spiritual attention this beatitude mandates. We physically attend to worship, but our minds are elsewhere; we try to pray, only to find we are not praying but pondering the next thing to do. We have full intentions to begin serving but find other things always take up our time.

In James 4:8, James says, "Get rid of your mixed motives, your duplicity, your double-mindedness; be simple and pure in your devotion."

As you pray, confess your lack of purity of heart, and ask God to give you focus.

Week 4

Today, I praise God for: _____

Read Matthew 5:9.

In a classic Winston Churchill story, Lady Astor once said, "If you were my husband, I'd put poison in your coffee." Churchill responded with his cutting wit: "If you were my wife, I'd drink it." This reveals that all of us are predisposed to conflict. In fact, some of us have clashed with so many people we don't really know how to live peaceably with others. Over the years, I have known some individuals who never seem happy unless they are fighting with someone.

Biblical peace is not merely the absence of activity. It is more than the absence of hostility (much deeper than just not having conflict). It is not just getting away from reality. Peace is not the absence of something bad; rather, it is the presence of something good. In the Old Testament, the word "peace" is "shalom" and is a state of wholeness and harmony intended to resonate in all relationships. When used as a greeting, shalom was a wish for outward freedom from disturbance as well as an inward sense of well-being. To a people constantly harassed by enemies, peace was the premiere blessing.

A true peacemaker is not passive, not caring what is going on around them. If there is a problem, the peacemaker admits it. Ezekiel warned against those who act as if all is well when it is not, who say, "'Peace' when there is not peace." Such people, according to Ezekiel, are merely plastering over cracked walls. Jeremiah said, "They dress the wound of my people as though it were not serious. 'Peace, peace,' they say, when there is no peace" (Jeremiah 6:14).

The peacemaker does not do this. The individual is painfully honest about the true status of relationships in the world, in the society in which he or she moves, and in his or her personal dealings. The peacemaker admits failed relationships and admits being at odds with others if it is so. The peacemaker honestly acknowledges tension if others have something against him or her. He or she does not pretend. The peacemaker refuses to say, "Peace, peace!" when there is no peace.

As you pray, is there a relationship in which you need to seek peace? If so, commit to do your part to bring peace.

Week 5

Today, I praise God for: _____

Read Matthew 5:13–16.

A *Peanuts* cartoon showed Peppermint Patty talking to Charlie Brown. She said, "Guess what, Chuck. The first day of school, and I got sent to the principal's office. It was your fault, Chuck." He said, "My fault? How could it be my fault? Why do you say everything is my fault?" She said, "You're my friend, aren't you, Chuck? You should have been a better influence on me."

While Peppermint Patty was seeking to pass the buck, she was in a very real sense right. We should be a good influence on our friends. Jesus is speaking about influence, and we live in a world that desperately needs to live the words of Jesus in this passage. Churches and individual Christians have stopped being salt and light, and our world reflects it. It is time that both of these are poured out.

What Jesus is telling the disciples is that as they live according to the beatitudes, people will be attracted to the Gospels. The difference will be evident, and they will desire to know what makes the Christian different. This is not a call to perfection (although that should not keep us from striving for it), nor does it require us to be "super spiritual." Rather, it demands we live differently from those around us and serve as an attractant for the Gospels.

Oliver Wendell Holmes put it this way: "I might have entered the ministry if certain preachers I knew had not acted and looked so much like undertakers." Some Christians behave as if they were baptized in lemon juice.

We must show by our lives that we are different. Are we rude and disrespectful? Do we go along with the crowd that ridicules someone while they are down? Do we give the best to those watching us, whether someone in line behind us at Walmart, another student at school, or a coworker? When we are respectful, courteous, considerate, and service-oriented, the world around us will see that Jesus really does make a difference.

If you answered yes to the questions above, confess those to the Lord, and ask Him to help you accept your role as salt and light, attracting people to Him.

Week 6

Today, I praise God for: _____

Read Matthew 5:21–26 and 2 Corinthians 5:16–21.

We all have times when we would like to grab someone by the neck and shake the person real good. There are even times when we would like to do more than shake them. When we are honest, there are people who feel the same way about us. That is the nature of relationships—people irritate us, and often they are the ones closest to us.

This problem is not new to us. It has been around since the creation of humankind. People have always rubbed each other wrong, conflict has arisen, and in many cases, hatred sets in. Jesus' original hearers felt like this was okay because in their eyes, they had not done anything wrong. They did not kill anyone, even if they wanted to, so they felt they were in good standing with the Lord. For the first time, Jesus points out He is concerned with the inner person rather than keeping a set of external rules.

A key truth all Christians need to understand is that human relationships greatly affect our heavenly relationship. This week's Scripture passage teaches that right relationships are void of anger and disrespect, and when a wrong occurs, Christians are to make amends quickly. This passage also instruct us to have right relationships in order to enhance our worship.

Perhaps you are sensing a dryness in your life. You pray, you try to be as religious and good as possible, but somehow it just does not seem to work. The reason might be that you have not faced up to your sin in a fundamental relationship.

This passage also leads us to purge ourselves of any delusion of spiritual superiority. It is all too true that a long association with Christ and His Word and church can foster the feeling of looking down on the rest of humanity as empty-headed and foolish. If there are those who ought to know who they are and what is within them, it is believers.

As you pray, ask God to convict you of broken relationships and empower you to seek reconciliation.

Week 7 ⟜

Today, I praise God for: _____

Read Matthew 6:27–30.

Bruce Larson tells of an old priest who was asked by a young man, "Father, when will I cease to be bothered by the sins of the flesh?" The priest replied, "Son, I wouldn't trust myself until I'd been dead for three or four days."

Jesus and His hearers lived in a Roman world where adultery was rampant. Roman men were known to have many mistresses, and the sentiment was that as long as you provided for your wife and children, you could have as many women as you liked. Adultery was no big deal. Jesus says it does not matter what your culture says about adultery; God still hates it.

In these verses, Jesus deals with a deeper issue than the act of adultery. His aim is to get at the root of adultery and frankly, the root of all sin, which is the spiritual condition of one's heart or mind. He says, "If anyone looks at a woman lustfully he has already committed adultery in his heart." A lustful, wicked heart is the real sin, Jesus says, not just the physical act of adultery itself. The word "lustful" here simply means "deep desire." Throughout the Bible, "lust" not only refers to sexual desire but to any insatiable hunger for pleasure, profit, power, or prestige. Lust is a desire for anything God forbids.

Jesus does not forbid the natural, normal attraction that is part of our humanity. What He forbids is deep-seated lust that consumes the inner person. It is not the first glance that is sin but the second that swells with lust and feeds upon the subject. The verb form Jesus uses stresses the fact the person has *already* committed adultery with the woman. It is an accomplished, irreversible fact.

Few male and female believers have not crossed the line from attraction to lust at some time. We are all adulterers by this standard. This realization ought to deliver us from all the judgmental behaviors toward those who have fallen to adultery. It should instill in us a poverty of spirit that realizes we are spiritually bankrupt and make us amazed that God loves us as He does.

Lust is usually a problem that begins with the thought life. The word "heart" in the Bible refers also to the mind. Here, Jesus talks about a man looking at a woman. It is not that the man just glances at her but that he fantasizes about having sex with her. His eyes see, his mind focuses, his body responds, and his thoughts go to gutter. He lusts. He has allowed his mind to wander and his heart to sin. He does not need to commit the physical act of adultery. He has done something worse; he has sinned in his heart. His heart is tainted.

Is the present evil world desensitizing us? Do things that once shocked us now pass us by with little notice? Have our sexual ethics slackened? Where do our minds wander when we have no duties to perform? What are we reading? Are there books, magazines, or computer files in our homes that we want no one else to see? How many adulteries did we watch last week? How many murders? How many did we watch with our children? How many chapters of the Bible did we read last week? Good questions. Pretty convicting.

Jesus calls us to extreme measures (29–30). It has been said that this line of discipline is the sternest one that ever struck humankind. Jesus is saying *anything* standing between us and Him must be ruthlessly torn out or cut off and thrown away.

John Stott says

If your eye causes you to sin because temptation comes to you through your eyes (objects you see), then pluck out your eyes. That is, don't look! Behave as if you had actually plucked out your eyes and flung them away, and were now blind and so could not see the object which previously caused you to sin. Again, if your hand or foot causes you to sin, because temptation comes to you through your hands (things you do) or your feet (places you visit), then cut them off. That is: Don't do it! Don't go! Behave as if you had actually cut off your hands and feet and had flung them away, and were now crippled and so could not do the things or visit the places which previously caused you to sin.

As you pray, if there is a temptation that has trapped you, you need to cut off its source. Make those commitments to the Lord. If you struggle with lust, cancel the movie stations. If you struggle with gossip, get off the phone or computer. If you struggle with alcohol, do not go to the bar for dinner. If you struggle with overeating, do not drive past the bakery seven times. Someone once said, "If you don't want to fall, don't walk where it's slippery." Cut off the source of your temptation.

Week 8

Today, I praise God for: _____

Read Matthew 5:33–37.

In the book *The Day America Told the Truth*, of those surveyed, 91 percent said they lie on a regular basis, 86 percent said they lie to their parents regularly, 75 percent said they lie to their friends, 69 percent said they lie to their spouses, and 50 percent said they regularly called in to work sick when they were not. They also found that almost as many Christians steal from work as non-Christians, are just as likely to falsify income taxes, steal time from work, and selectively obey the law.

We get to the point where we lie without even thinking about it: "I will be at church tomorrow." "Officer, I did not know I was speeding." "That bill has been paid; it must be lost in the mail." "You can count on me to …" Politicians have lied, spouses have lied, parents have lied—we have been effected by every sphere of life, and so were Jesus' hearers.

Oaths were encouraged in the Old Testament. Deuteronomy 10:20

says, "Fear the Lord your God and serve him. Hold fast to him and take your oaths in His name." They were not only encouraged to make oaths and vows but to do so in God's name!

What was discouraged was making a vow, swearing to do something, and then not doing it. Moses repeatedly emphasized this: "Do not swear falsely by My name and so profane the name of God. I am the Lord" (Lev. 19:12). "When a man makes a vow to the Lord or takes an oath to obligate himself by a pledge, he must not break His word but must do everything he said" (Num. 30:2). Oaths were encouraged, but once made, they were not to be broken under any circumstances. The Bible teaches that oaths are serious business. Jesus calls His people to keep their word.

As you pray, commit to living a life marked by truthfulness and confess areas of falsehood. We are to follow the truth, tell the truth, and live the truth.

Week 9 ⟨⟩

Today, I praise God for: _____

Read Matthew 5:38–48.

In June 2010, Detroit Tigers pitcher Armando Galarraga was on the verge of history, needing one more out to complete the 21st perfect game in baseball—no hits, no walks, no errors, no hit batters. The final batter hit a routine ground ball but hustled to first base, making the play close. First base umpire, Jim Joyce, called him safe, but replays show the hitter was clearly out. Galarraga's perfect game was ruined. Chaos ensued on the field and in the media as Joyce admitted he missed the call. The next day, Joyce was the home plate umpire and entered the field in tears, moved by the cheers of the crowd. Galarraga took the lineup card to Joyce. As the two men reached home plate, the scene was remarkable. They shook hands and patted each other on the back. It was selfless, generous, and loving, and it is how we are to respond to those who hurt us.

What this means for us is that when we are insulted or abused for Christ's sake (not when it is because of wrong we have done), we must not respond by getting even. We must turn the other cheek. Jesus calls us to swallow our pride and give up our "right" to get even. In effect, Jesus is saying that in turning the other cheek, you make the other person and his or her well-being the center of your focus. We think of them and adjust our actions according to what we think will point them to Christ.

If you impartially show love to your enemies as well as to friends, you will be like God, who shows the impartiality of His love by sending the sun and rain on both the righteous and the unrighteous. When we love without limits, we are like God. Jesus' point is that even those disgusting, double-crossing tax collectors loved their own tax-gathering buddies. So if a person loves only his friends, he is doing no better than a dwindling tax collector. You love your friend who reciprocates your love. Big deal. Followers of Jesus should do *more* than what is common among nonbelievers in the way they show love. It is this "more" that is the distinctive quality of the Christian's love. The call is to practice unlimited love.

As you pray, commit to practice the love of God, seeking forgiveness for the lack of responding in His love.

Week 10 ⟨⟩

Today, I praise God for: _____

Read Matthew 6:1–4.

There is a lot of pretending in life. In a college town, a bar frequented by students ran the following ad in the campus paper during the days before Parents Weekend: "Bring Your Parents for Lunch Saturday. We'll Pretend We Don't Know You!" The ad was soon challenged by a college minister, who posted a revised version on the campus bulletin board. It read, "Bring Your Parents to Church Sunday. We'll Pretend We Know You!"

There is a lot of pretending in life, isn't there? We have heroes we almost worship only to find out they were pretending to be someone they were not. We have political leaders who claim to be champions of the poor only to find out they are using the poor for votes. There are many young women who go out with guys who pretend to love them, so they can get what they really want from them. People use people to get what they want. Maybe some of you have felt that sting. In life, people are looking for something real to hold on to. People are looking for people who are genuine, and Jesus is also looking for those people.

During Jesus' day, many people were going through the motions of religion, so they would receive accolades from other people. The Pharisees, for instance, practiced a performance-oriented righteousness focused on deeds, without regard for any relationship. To Jesus, this was unacceptable. Jesus tells us that if we do things to receive attention from people, we will have received our reward. It is possible to be a modern-day Good Samaritan and have no reward from God. It is possible to pray for our enemies and have no reward. It is possible to sing or preach like an angel and have no reward. Why? Because it is possible to do all these things for the recognition of people and not of God.

I find this terrifying because it means that my life, which is given to God, can in the end count for nothing. The most outwardly, godly saint in our church may have all "good deeds" rejected.

As you pray, consider if you seek the recognition of God or people.

Week 11 ⟨‿‿⟩

Today, I praise God for: _____

Read Matthew 6:5–8.

The hypocrites liked to engage in public prayer in two places—on street corners and in the synagogues. Each afternoon during the temple sacrifice and public fasts, trumpets were blown as a sign it was time to pray. Wherever a devout man was on the street, he stopped, faced the temple, and prayed. It was a perfect opportunity to let everyone see your stuff. You could time your afternoon stroll so that you were on a very prominent corner when the trumpet sounded, and you could lift your hands and pray for all to hear.

Prayer in the synagogue was led by a member of the congregation who stood before the ark of the Law, raised his hands, and prayed. It was easy to become preachy, using all the right clichés, dramatic pauses, and voice variations to impress the crowds.

Jesus was not condemning public prayer. He was condemning the desire to be *seen* praying publicly. The early church thrived on prayer, as the opening chapters of Acts show. Jesus was emphasizing that prayer is essentially a conversation between the believer and God. It is private, not something to put on display. One is to shut out every distraction and focus on God.

The Lord was not and is not impressed with a lot of words. He is impressed with what the *heart* is saying. Our sin is so entrenched that one can easily find himself pouring out his soul to God, only to have the prayer dissolve into preoccupation with self so that he is really worshiping himself. Sadly, innumerable prayers, public and private, never rise beyond self.

Some questions to consider: Do I pray frequently or more fervently when I am alone with God than when I am in public? Is my public praying an overflow of my private prayer? What do I think of when I am praying in public? Am I looking for "just the right" phrase? Am I thinking of the worshipper more than of God? Is it possible that the reason more of my prayers are not answered is because I am more concerned about bringing my prayer to people than to God?

As you pray, shut out every distraction, focus on God, and pour out your heart.

Week 12

Today, I praise God for: _____

Read Matthew 6:25–34.

Half of all the people in America's hospital beds are constant worriers. Forty-three percent of all adults suffer health effects due to worry and stress. Between 75 percent and 90 percent of all visits to primary-care physicians are stress-related complaints or disorders. Worry has been linked to all the leading causes of death, including heart disease, cancer, lung ailments, accidents, cirrhosis, and suicide. An estimated 1 million workers are absent on an average workday because of stress-related complaints. Stress is said to be responsible for more than half of the 550 million workdays lost annually because of absenteeism. Mental distress can lead to death. Add to the list the mental fatigue of nights without sleep and days without peace, and we get a glimpse of the havoc worry plays in destroying the quality and quantity of life.

Jesus tells us three times in this passage not to worry. We might think, *I know Jesus said that, but it is impossible.* If He commanded it, it can be followed. He gets our attention here because He uses words that cite the world's largest concern—what we eat, drink, and wear. Self-indulgence is what our culture is all about, and that is why there is so much anxiety. We reduce ourselves to being just bodies that need to be fed, watered, clothed, and housed. Since life itself comes directly from God, why should we worry about His giving us the food and drink necessary for life? He will not go halfway. He gave you life, and He will maintain it as long as He wills. When we believe there is a God who has given us the great gift of life, we do not need to be anxious about the little things we need daily.

What Jesus did *not* mean needs to be said, too. He was not calling us to laziness. Birds instinctively make provision for the future. It has been said that no creature works harder than birds. The example of the birds does not teach that if we trust God, every day will be smooth sailing. Birds sometimes starve, are eaten by predators, and certainly die in a short span. The birds demonstrate God's care for the lower creation, so we, who are a much higher creation, can be assured of His great care. Birds do not have a father; only we can call God Father. The birds do not bear His image; we do! "Are you not much more valuable than they?" is an understatement.

As you pray, confess areas of worry, and replace them with faith.

Week 13 ⌇⟋⟍⟍⟍⟍⟍⟍⟍⟍⟍⟍⟍⟍⟍⟍⟍⟍⟍⟍⟍⟍⟍⟍⟍⟍⟍⟍⟍

Today, I praise God for: _____

Read Matthew 7:1–5.

Criticism boosts our own self-image. Pointing out someone else's failure and tearing him or her down seem to build us up, at least in our own eyes. Criticism is an enjoyed pastime. There is a tendency in human nature to take pleasure in hearing and sharing bad news and shortcomings. Criticism makes us feel our own lives (morality and behavior) are better than the person who failed. Criticism helps us justify the decisions we made and the things we have done throughout our lives. We rationalize our actions by pointing out the failure of others. Criticism points out to our friends how strong we are. Criticism gives us good feelings because our rigid beliefs and strong lives are proven again by comparing our lives to another's failure. Criticism is an outlet for hurt and revenge. We feel they deserve it. "He hurt me so he deserves to hurt, too." So we criticize the person who failed.

Christians have an obligation to exercise critical judgment, referred to as discernment. There is a universe of difference between being discerning and being critical. A discerning spirit is constructive; a critical spirit is destructive. The person with a destructive, critical spirit enjoys his or her position and expects to find fault.

When King David was at the lowest moral point in his life—having committed adultery with Uriah's wife, discovering she was pregnant, and then having Uriah killed—Nathan the prophet told him a story about a rich man with huge flocks of sheep who lived next door to a poor man. The poor man had only one ewe lamb that he loved like a daughter. The rich man, not wanting to take a lamb out of his own herds to feed some guests, took the little lamb and slaughtered it. David's response was basically, "That man deserves to die. He must repay everything fourfold." Nathan, pointing a prophetic finger at the king, pronounced, "You are that man!" Forget someone else's speck, look at the log in your own eye, David.

We find it so easy to turn a microscope on another person's sin while we look at ours through the wrong end of a telescope. We use some strong terms for someone else's sin but an excuse for our own. We easily spot a speck of phoniness in another because we have a logjam of it in our own lives.

As you pray, ask God to remove any condemning judgment concerning others.

Week 14

Today, I praise God for: _____

Read Matthew 7:7–8 and Luke 11:5–13

Holocaust survivor Corrie Ten Boom once said, "When a Christian shuns fellowship with other Christians, the devil smiles. When he stops studying the Bible, the devil laughs. When the stops praying, the devil shouts for joy."

Jesus teaches that we are to pray with persistence. Ask, seek, and knock indicate a rising scale of intensity in one's prayers and points to the persistent manner of life lived before the Father. "Ask" indicates coming to God with humility and consciousness of a need, as a child fittingly comes to her father. "Seek" involves asking but adds action; it links one's prayer with responsible activity in pursuing God's will, as when a person prays for a job and at the same time checks out leads. "Knock" includes perseverance in one's asking and seeking, as when someone perseveres in praying for his or her unbelieving family's salvation and speaks and lives the gospel throughout one's lifetime.

Literally, the text says "keep on asking … keep on seeking … keep on knocking." Jesus' disciples are to ask the Father continually in a manner of life to be constantly responsible in pursuing God's will, and to maintain an unremitting determination in expecting the Father to answer.

Some situations require more than merely asking for something. Seeking, then, is not a simple act; it is a process, a series of acts. This knocking is not a single rap; it is a series of raps. It is a request for admission, repeated if necessary, and suggests situations where we seek an entrance or an opportunity.

None of us will ever understand God's timing, because it rarely matches our own. It is easy to give up on praying when the results are lacking, but we must remember God will not respond until He is ready—and we are ready. Persistent prayer prepares us.

As you pray, consider areas of need that you have not been persistent in prayer and plead for God to answer.

Week 15

Today, I praise God for: _____

Read Nehemiah 1:1–11.

Nehemiah opens with some brief but important information. Nehemiah is living in a fortified city and is greeted by some close associates. What follows reveals Nehemiah's heart. His people, the Israelites, had survived the Babylonian captivity and returned to Jerusalem. They were in "great trouble and disgrace." The city was defenseless. A delegation of his people came from Jerusalem to ask him to ask the king to take action to relieve the sufferings of God's people. Nehemiah's burden became increasingly overwhelming as he began to realize God wanted to use him to bring deliverance.

Nehemiah had a concern for others, and he heard and received the truth that things were bad. He responded in a personal way: he sat down and wept. "For some days" he wept, prayed, and fasted, which may have lasted three or four months. When we mourn, we know our hearts are broken; when we fast and pray, we know we have become deeply involved and concerned.

Nehemiah had plenty of reasons to lose faith. God's people were scattered, the city of God was destroyed, and God's chosen children were living defenseless. However, he still believed God to be God! Nehemiah says: God is still God; seek Him while He may be found!

Don't lose faith! He is the God who keeps His covenant of love with those who love Him and obey His commands.

I ask you today to consider areas where your heart needs to break for people in need. There are many people in our community who are like Nehemiah's people; they in great trouble and disgrace. Some need a personal relationship with Jesus, while others need to experience deep repentance. These are your family members, friends, neighbors, classmates, coworkers—people you know personally.

As you pray, ask God to break your heart over those with spiritual needs. Just as Nehemiah looked for the opportunity to share with the king, ask the Lord to open your eyes to opportunities to share with those in need about the King of Kings. Pray for these individuals specifically as God brings them to your heart.

Week 16

Today, I praise God for: _____

Read Ephesians 1:15–23.

A crowded flight was canceled. A single agent was rebooking a long line of inconvenienced travelers. Suddenly, an angry passenger pushed his way to the desk. He slapped his ticket down on the counter and said, "I *have* to be on this flight, and it has to be first class." The agent replied, "I'm sorry, sir. I'll be happy to try to help you, but I've got to help these folks first. And I'm sure we'll be able to work something out." The passenger was unimpressed. He asked loudly so that the passengers behind him could hear, "Do you have any idea who I am?" Without hesitating, the gate agent smiled and grabbed her public address microphone. "May I have your attention, please?" she began, her voice bellowing throughout the terminal. "We have a passenger here at the gate who does not know who he is. If anyone can help him find his identity, please come to the gate."

It is important to know who we are. As believers in Jesus Christ, there is a vast expanse of entitlements not available to those who do not have a personal relationship with Jesus. One of those is that we can approach the throne of God in prayer on behalf of others.

Paul writes this letter from a prison cell, and he understood the importance of the church being a praying people. The church is not an independent, self-determining group; it is a community that acknowledges it is owned by God and, therefore, under one direction. Our regular practice should include praying for other Christians- even ones we do not know. Through such prayers, we acknowledge we all belong to the same God and participate together in a common, God-given mission.

I believe we fail to pray for others, as Paul did, because we would rather God use us than them. Do you thrill of hearing of the faith and love of others? Do we praise God when He works in places we are not present? Other churches? It is a fact that only those who are thankful for the spiritual growth of others can truly pray for them.

As you pray, who in your life needs you to pray for them? Celebrate what God is doing in the lives of those within your church. Pray for the persecuted church scattered across the world.

Week 17

Today, I praise God for: _____

Read Ephesians 2:19–22.

Citizenship was a great source of pride in the ancient world. It was highly personal and provided one's identity. The laws and customs were part of one's being, and a lifelong connection was established between inhabitants. Paul was telling the Ephesian Christians that they had come to possess a citizenship far superior to any local citizenship and even the coveted Roman citizenship.

Before coming to Christ, they lived in alienation, but now they were reconciled to God and belonged. When we trust in Christ, we become a common people. We have a common language, heritage, and history as part of the community of faith. We have a common allegiance that supersedes all loyalties. We have a common goal—glorifying God. We have the same destination—a place prepared by Christ—and, "our citizenship is in heaven."

Paul speaks of the family as a building with a strong foundation, God's Word. The church stands or falls in its regard for the Word. If we tamper with the foundation, the temple will crumble. That is why Paul ordered Timothy to "preach the Word" (2 Tim. 4:2).

Important as the foundation is, there is another component of even greater importance, and that is the cornerstone, Christ Jesus Himself. The cornerstone determines the stability of the foundation and the character of the entire building. The lay of the walls, the dimensions of the structure result from the chief cornerstone. All other stones had to be adjusted to it.

The final piece is us, the building blocks. We have a beautiful image of the new temple, God's people. Picture Jesus as the massive cornerstone. Next the foundational teaching of the New Testament is laid upon and around Him. He gives it its shape and stability, and the whole foundation assumes His glow. Then one by one, living stones are set upon it.

As you pray, thank God that our citizenship is in heaven through our inclusion into the family of God. Commit to adjusting your life to the chief cornerstone.

Week 18 ⟨⎯⎯⎯⟩
Today, I praise God for: _____

Read Ephesians 3:1–11

This is a great passage that gives the characteristics of those who are called. We will only look at one, found in verse 1: a prisoner of Christ.

Paul was in prison in Rome when he wrote Ephesians. He did not consider himself a prisoner of Rome but one of Christ Jesus, because it was out of obedience to Jesus that he was imprisoned. He trusted completely in the sovereignty of God. He considered his circumstances to be God's will, so the gospel could be spread to the Gentiles.

A prisoner has no rights; you are told what you can do, when you can do it. Paul is saying that he has relinquished the rights to his personal life. He is now focused on doing what God has called him to do, when He called him to do it, and how God told him to do it. He was in jail for preaching the gospel, and all he had to do to stay out was leave town or change the message. But he was a prisoner of Christ long before a Roman prisoner, so Paul followed God's call to preach to the Gentiles.

Many prisoners maintain their innocence, but Paul accepted his responsibility and continued to praise God and tell about Him in jail. Why? Because he had died to himself and lived for Christ, which involved losing his personal rights and being a prisoner for Christ.

As Americans, we treasure the rights we have as a result of our citizenship—for example, freedom of speech, to bear arms, and against unlawful search and seizure. But as children of God, we do not have rights. Our lives Are to be about living according to God's will, fulfilling the responsibilities He gives, and bringing honor to Him through how we live. Notice there is nothing about us!

As you pray, consider if are you still holding certain areas of your life hostage, or have you given up your rights and admitted you are a prisoner of Christ?

Week 19 ⟨⟩

Today, I praise God for: _____

Read Ephesians 3:14–16

Paul is moved to his knees in this prayer, which is remarkable in the fact that it was not customary for Jews to kneel in prayer. The ordinary posture was standing, just as many continue to do today before the Wailing Wall in Jerusalem, rocking back and forth as they say their prayers. Kneeling indicated an extraordinary event or an unusual passion, such as Solomon at the dedication of the temple, Jesus in the garden, and Paul when he made his tearful good-bye to the elders in Ephesus.

Paul was moved to kneel for at least two reasons. First, because of the stunning impact on himself of the immense revelation he delivered. Second, because of his relationship with his Father. Paul knew he was loved, and that put him on his knees. He used Abba, "Daddy," which Jews considered to be too familiar to use in relation to God without qualification. The barrier was down, and Paul was moved to humility and fell to his knees in prayer. We would do good to learn from his example and remember the need to rid ourselves of pride in praying. And it has nothing to do with one's physical position.

Paul prays to be strengthened. Just as an ill person needs to be strengthened so they can take in all life has to offer, so also God's children need to be inwardly strengthened to receive all the blessings God has for them and to be used in all the ways God ordains. This is a fundamental work of God from His Spirit to our spirit. Paul prays we would be strengthened in the face of our weaknesses by the power of God. Power is not meant to be corralled or saved for a rainy day; it is meant to be used to change something. To impact something. To be implemented and used to make a difference.

It is futile to come to a pauper with our requests, no matter how moving and passionate the appeal may be. But to come before the One from whom are all things and to whom are all things makes for great optimism, especially when He is no mere Rockefeller who gave *from* his riches, but is rather the One who gives *according to* His riches.

Pray for strength through the power of God, that you will be a frail container, pulsating with divine power.

Week 20 ⸻

Today, I praise God for: _____

Read Ephesians 4:17–24.

This passage presents a divine wardrobe that we wear when our lives are changed by Christ. This is a heavenly, eternal style that will never go out of date, a wardrobe that wears increasingly better with time.

Tragically, the old wardrobe is just as much in style today as it was in Paul's day. The Gentiles in Ephesus were particularly sinful. There was temple prostitution, crime, idolatry, and every other kind of sin. Many Christians in Ephesus came from that background, so Paul appeals, "Do not live like that any longer!"

Paul calls Ephesian Christians, and us, to "put off your old self." When we are changed through the forgiveness and grace of Jesus, we remove our old clothing and put on new clothes. The two cannot be worn together.

The instruction that Paul gives is a challenge to repeatedly put off the old garments, the old style of life. Scripture and experience teach us no one has ever succeeded in shedding the garments of the old life with a single, unrepeated action. Those who live holy lives do so by repeated putting off their old way. The problem is, the old garments are so comfortable and natural. Not only that, many have worn them for so long that they naturally drape over us, and we barely know we are wearing them until the Holy Spirit corrects us. Our sins will have to be put off daily as long as we live.

As you pray, inspect your life to see if you have put on some of your old clothes. Ask God to reveal if you have picked up old clothes that you once discarded. As God corrects, remove these clothes, and experience the cleansing of the Lord.

Week 21

Today, I praise God for: _____

Read Ephesians 4:29 and James 3:9–12.

As Paul talks about the change that occurs in the life of one who trusts Christ for salvation, he concludes that there should be a difference with their words. The language Paul uses is very descriptive. "Unwholesome talk" literally means "rotten, putrid, or filthy." This includes obscene language, but the emphasis is on decay-spreading conversation that runs down others and delights in their weaknesses. Gossip, slander, and similar sins fall into Paul's instruction.

A person who engages in this is like the fabled slave who took poison into her system a little at a time, and then more and more, until at last her whole being was so full of poison her very breath withered flowers. There are Christians who become like this; wicked speech comes as naturally as breathing. Such talk must not be part of the believer's life.

Paul concludes with the imperative that we are to speak, "only what is helpful for building others up according to their needs, that it may benefit those who listen." The word "benefit" literally means "grace." We are to converse in such a way that our words become a vehicle and demonstration of the grace of God.

James states that just as freshwater and saltwater cannot come from the same spring, out of the mouth of the child of God cannot come "praise and cursing." We cannot talk about the goodness of God one minute and the failures of our brothers and sisters the next. It is unnatural.

As you pray, ask God to forgive you of the sins of the tongue, including (but not limited to) cursing, lying, and gossiping. Ask for the strength you need to control your tongue and use it to build up others.

Week 22 ⌣⟶

Today, I praise God for: _____

Read Ephesians 5:15–20.

Paul calls Christians to live their lives with care. Literally, "watch carefully [or closely] how you walk." The word translated "carefully" carries the connotation of something done accurately, precisely, or given close attention. The phrase suggests a purpose and direction to life. Life is not aimless. Nor is it a series of frantic activities followed by downtime, although that is the normal pattern for the American life. Life is the steady progress toward the goal.

The call to live wisely is not a call for theoretical knowledge. It is a call for moral discernment and a practical skill in making decisions. The emphasis remains on the mind and on careful attention to keep life on target, the target being what pleases Christ and fits His purposes. There is attention to detail, similar to searching for something you know is in a general area.

If you have named Jesus Christ Lord and believed He died for you and rose again so He could be your salvation and life, it ought to make a difference in how you live. You live carefully, manage your time, watch your steps, control your tongue, and so on.

The problem is that many Christians understand their salvation as more a matter of receiving eternal life *from* Christ than of giving our temporal lives *to* Christ. Yet both must be true. We can easily develop the habit of being in charge of our own lives instead of placing our lives in the hands of God. At some point, if our lives are going to take on a likeness to Christ and be fruitful for God, we must reach a major milestone commitment and give our all to Him. That commitment will make us reevaluate everything we do.

Paul says to "make the most of every opportunity," an interpretation of the phrase, "redeeming the time." We are to buy up every opportunity. Time is going by, and evil will use it if Christians do not. The opposite of redeeming time is losing time. This verse reflects an urgency about life. Time is important and ought not be wasted.

Are you living carefully, looking for ways to make the most of every opportunity? If not, repent that you are wasting your life.

Week 23 ⌣⟩

Today, I praise God for: _____

Read Ephesians 5:21–6:4 and John 13

Many are offended by the word "submission," as if it points to a passive, weak life dominated by a negative self-image, a giving up of control and free will. This is not Paul's intent, except for the fact that control for Christians has already been given over to Christ.

It is important to note this text does not ask some Christians to submit to other Christians. It asks all Christians to submit to each other. No privileged group is in view.

Submission is the self-giving love, humility, and willingness to die that is demanded of all Christians. Jesus said it this way: "Whoever exalts himself will be humbled, and whoever humbles himself will be exalted." Without mutual submission, we cannot be filled with the Spirit.

Sometimes we meet Christians who claim to be Spirit-filled but are brash, assertive, and self-promoting. Thus they give their claim the lie, for neither Christ nor the Holy Spirit like this.

John 13 is a great picture of submission, along with Jesus' words in 13:14–16. He used the logic if it is true for the greater (me), it is true for the lesser (you).

Paul applies the command of submission to the family. The wife should submit to the husband, the husband must sacrifice for the wife, the children must obey their parents, and the parents must train their children. While submission is only used one time, "sacrifice," "obey," and "train" are ways submission is shown.

The home that God blesses is the one that follows the model Paul teaches. As you pray, consider your role(s) in your home, and ask God to convict you of times when you fail to "submit to one another out of reverence for Christ." Plead for God to do a supernatural work in your family as a whole and in the life of each individual.

Week 24

Today, I praise God for: _____

Read Numbers 13:26–14:10.

As the nation of Israel neared the Promised Land, spies were sent to investigate the land. The whole nation was awaiting the return of the spies and their report. They believed their leaders would never mislead them. The spies may have selected a spokesman, or it may have been ten of them together who concluded the land could not be taken. The people were immediately riled up. We don't know what may have been said between verses 29 and 30 in chapter 13, but after the majority give their reports, notice Caleb in verse 30 says, "We should go up and take possession of the land, for we can *certainly* do it." It is as if Caleb shouts, "Let's roll!" but turns around to find that no one is going with him.

Caleb immediately knows he is outnumbered. The spies, who were trusted for their credibility, exaggerated to the people. Where the people were, geological excavations have shown parts of the area were not inhabited, and the area included in their report is larger than they were instructed to explore.

Where is Joshua? He agrees with Caleb, but because he is Moses' assistant, everyone knows he has vested interests. Caleb, however, could easily have sided with the majority. A landslide vote could not even shake his determination to follow the Lord.

Caleb stands in the face of opposition because he is confident of his assertion due to the fact that "the Lord is with us." The whole assembly talked about stoning them, and I figure that was talked about from the start. Yet Caleb remained strong and was one of two, along with Joshua, who were allowed to live to see the Promised Land.

As you commit to a godly live, you will encounter opposition. Ask God to give you the strength to stand in the face of opposition and remain committed to His call on your life, trusting in the reward of God.

Week 25 ⟮⟶⟯

Today, I praise God for: _____

Read Joshua 2.

There are many surprising twists and turns in the story of taking the Promised Land, but God is with them all the way. When the spies arrive, they encountered a most unexpected situation. However, they found themselves right where God wanted them to be—in the home of a prostitute.

Why would God choose a prostitute? Wasn't there a righteous person in Jericho he could have picked? Jericho was part of the Amorite kingdom, a grotesquely violent, totally depraved, thoroughly pagan culture so hellbent on the pursuit of everything evil, that God Himself had condemned them and ordered the Israelites to wipe them from the face of the earth. Rahab's life modeled the life of the culture, her livelihood dependent on evil.

Why didn't God just wipe them all out and let the people enter? That is where grace enters the picture. While God is going to punish Jericho for its sin, He is also going to show grace toward someone who does not deserve it. That is what makes it grace.

You may be struggling with, "Can God forgive me/use me after all I have done?" You have seen more than your share of spiritual pigpens. Some have done things you would not want the person next to you to know about. There's a segment of your life you would not want made into a movie. You have tried to erase it from your memory bank, but every so often, Satan throws it back in your face, "Remember when …"

God used Rahab, a prostitute, and He will use you. Others may not forgive, accept, or even tolerate you, but God does, because God has more grace than people do.

As you pray, accept the fact that through His forgiveness, God can use you despite your past. Celebrate the power of God that Rahab described in Joshua 2:9–11. Ask the Lord to search your heart and convict you of times when you believe He cannot use other individuals because of their pasts.

Week 26 ⟨⟩

Today, I praise God for: _____

Read 2 Samuel 23:8–17.

This passage is about David's "Mighty Men," the best warriors to serve in his army. David was in a cave and longed for some water. But not just any water; some water from Bethlehem. It was a huge risk for these three men to get the water—walk twelve miles, sneak through enemy troops, approach the main gate of an occupied city, lower a bucket silently into the well. Then they had to do it all over again, this time carrying a jug of water. It doesn't sound like a walk in the park. Then again, if it was easy, everyone would have been doing it.

When was the last time you took a risk? You probably took many more risks when you were younger. It seems like the older we get, the more comfortable the cave seems and the more dangerous the road to Bethlehem looks. Life is about taking risks; it should not be about playing it safe. Every noteworthy contribution ever made to society started as a risk.

Imagine how different the Bible would be without risks. What if Abraham had said no when told to leave all he had to pursue the vision of a great nation—especially when told you will be the father of a nation when you aren't even the father of a child. What would have happened if Noah had decided to play it safe and not become a boat builder? And if David decided that tending sheep had a better future than fighting giants? What if Daniel realized it was safer to obey the king's command than to pray? If Mary had told the angel she didn't really want to be a teenage mom? What if Jesus had come to the conclusion there was a brighter future in being a carpenter than being the Messiah? If Henry Ford hadn't taken a risk, would we still be riding horses? If Edison hadn't taken a risk, would we still be reading by candles? If Graham Bell hadn't taken a risk, would we be living with the telephone?

The face of the earth and the scope of human history have been changed by those who were willing to take a risk. While we can't all be Fords and Edisons, every one of us has the ability to change our world. We all have the ability to leave a mark with our lives. But only if we are willing to take a risk.

What risk do you need to take? Commit it to the Lord.

Week 27 ⟨ ➞

Today, I praise God for: _____

Read 2 Samuel 6:12–23.

This passage examines the time David's worship got out of control, and he danced naked before the Lord. No one wants you to follow this example completely, but each of us should pray our worship is an active response to God, whereby we declare His worth.

As we come to corporate or family worship, may we only care about the audience we have with the Lord and not on pleasing those around us. There are times when we will experience true worship only to have someone complain about something, and the worship comes to a screeching halt. That is what happened with David due to his wife, Michal.

Michal observed worship without experiencing worship; she, "watched from a window" (16). She saw the activity of worship as a threat to personal dignity and public decorum. "She despised him in her heart" (16). She rejects the legitimacy of any act of worship (20c). David had removed all of the kingly ornaments he wore for a linen ephod, a priestly garment connected with seeking a word from God. It would be similar to an apron or a loincloth.

Michal is described as "Saul's daughter," not "David's wife." She may have loved David, but she didn't love his God; she acted like her father, not her husband. While nation and king celebrate the joyous occasion, Michal sulks as though Saul would have done better.

Michal was too worried about her appearance to others to join in the worship. David, though, was only worried about his audience of One. He did not care what anyone else thought.

As you pray, prepare for your audience of One.

Week 28 ⌣͡⟶

Today, I praise God for: _____

Read Genesis 3:1–13.

We live in a word of excuses. Here are some complied by *Readers Digest* that have been offered for not showing up for work: "I dreamed I was fired, so I didn't want to get out of bed"; "I was up all night arguing with God"; "A raccoon stole my work shoe off my porch"; "I wasn't thinking and accidentally went to my old job"; "While rowing across the river to work, I got lost in the fog"; "I didn't have money for gas, because all the pawnshops were closed"; "My dog dialed 911, and the police wanted to question me about what 'really' happened."

Maybe you have not used excuses to this degree, but if we are honest, we are all susceptible to making them and passing the blame. This has been a part of humankind since the fall. In the passage today, you might have thought of the long-time excuse, "The woman made me do it!" Men have probably been laughing about this since the first time someone read the story of Adam and Eve. Adam blames Eve, and Eve blames the Serpent. We have followed a similar course.

We normally see this encounter as Eve eating the fruit, finding Adam, and then sharing with him. Notice, though, "She also gave some to her husband, who was with her, and he ate it." Adam was there the whole time, refusing to take a stand. His refusal to speak up is seen as support for Eve's actions.

Where in your life do you act as Adam, passively watching and not speaking up? It may be as you watch your spouse make ungodly choices. I regularly see parents act in this manner, refusing to address sin in their children's life out of fear of what they will think. We laugh at the decisions of our friends rather than having our hearts break at the ungodly choices they make. It is time to speak up.

Where do you need to ask for forgiveness due to standing by and watching sin take place? Ask God to give you the strength to quit giving excuses and be marked by obedience and faithfulness.

Week 29 ⌒⟩

Today, I praise God for: _____

Read Genesis 4.

Frank Sinatra recorded "My Way," written by Paul Anka, in 1968. Many who knew Sinatra suspected the song was part music and part autobiography. The lyrics sound like the determined voice of a man who had experienced a lot of ups and downs in life. Even when life didn't turn out the way he wanted, he stood his ground. No one was going to tell him what to do. Here is the opening verse: "And now, the end is here And so I face the final curtain/My friend, I'll say it clear I'll state my case, of which I'm certain/I've lived a life that's full I traveled each and ev'ry highway/And more, much more than this, I did it my way."

As Cain and Abel made preparations and then gathered for worship, Cain's motto could have been, "I did it my way." Much has been made through the years regarding why God accepted Abel's sacrifice but not Cain's. The New Testament explains the difference between Cain and Abel this way. Hebrews 11:4 says, "By faith Abel offered God a better sacrifice than Cain did. By faith he was commended as a righteous man, when God spoke well of his offerings." God rejected Cain's character as well as his sacrifice. Abel's offering was the overflow of a believing life. Cain went through the motions. His heart was not in it. His life didn't back up his actions. God knows the difference, even when others do not.

Cain knew God was not pleased. What is a person do when that happens? One can own up to the problem. An individual can acknowledge the error, ask for forgiveness, and pledge to do better the next time. Or the person can get mad, blame God, and feel sorry for himself or herself. That's the way of Cain. The Lord gave Cain a warning in verses 6 and 7. No one toys with sin and wins. Insisting on doing life our way doesn't make us free. It simply produces a less merciful master.

As you examine your life, what areas are not pleasing to God? Will you respond like Cain, or will you acknowledge your sin, seek God's forgiveness, and commit to living God's way? How you address this area of your life is a key to whether you will lead your family in godliness.

Week 30

Today, I praise God for: _____

Read Genesis 6.

Living in a democratic nation, we are used to majority rule. The majority, though, is not always right. Most of the people in Germany thought Hitler was right when World War II broke out. Most of the people in the South thought slavery was right when the Civil War was fought. The majority was not right.

Noah was not in the majority. The human race was marked by wickedness and thought of evil "all the time." Noah had resisted being caught in this trap, resulting in favor in the eyes of the Lord. He did not fit in to the society in which he lived, because "he walked faithfully with God." His life was marked by obedience not wickedness.

There were probably people who never saw anyone live as Noah lived. All they ever knew was wickedness. Noah lived unlike any other person.

When the Lord called Noah to build an ark to save himself and his family, "Noah did everything just as God commanded him." Think about it. It has never rained, and the Lord had never commanded anyone to build such a vessel. Noah was called to do something that had never been done before, and he responded with obedience.

Most Christians are afraid of having a similar encounter with the Lord, of being called to do something they have never done before or something they have never known to have been done before. We like the ordinary. We prefer proof that something can succeed. We like to play it safe.

Noah started to work, building the ark to the exact specifications that God commanded because he knew of no other way to respond than obedience.

Is God calling you to something you have never done before? Why have you not been obedient? Confess this to Him, along with your fears, and ask for the courage to be obedient.

Week 31 ⌣⟩

Today, I praise God for: _____

Read Genesis 12:1–9.

Annie Taylor was the first person to survive going over Niagara Falls. In 1901, the sixty-three-year-old teacher used an oak barrel packed with inflated pillows. She was fished out bruised and shaken but alive. Her first words to onlookers were, "No one ought to ever do that again."

Attempting to conquer Niagara Falls is risk-taking without reason. Many call is stupidity. In contrast, Abram took a step of faith. God called him to leave his land and go "to the land I will show you." He had to decide whether to abandon all he knew in favor of the land God offered, which Abram knew nothing about. He had to decide whether to set aside his blessing, his inheritance, for the inheritance God describes. The offer was much, but the cost was high.

God made a great promise to Abram: "I will bless you … you will be a blessing … all people will be blessed through you." In order to experience the blessing, he had to leave. Leave what is for what will be, resting completely upon the naked promise of God. Notice that when the Lord called Abram, Abram was comfortable. Everything was fine in his world. He was content with his life. But God shook him up.

One of the reasons our churches need revival is because we get comfortable with life. We get accustomed to an area of sinfulness. We are happy with our service. The status quo is enjoyable. We find lots of support because no one wants a loved one to be uncomfortable.

A common fear is that we will have to quit our job, sell the house, and move to a distant country. The rich young ruler was told he must sell all he had and give the money to the poor. God does not ask that of all of us, but to be a true disciple, we have to be willing to leave anything we are asked to leave. It might be a job, but it could also be a habit, an attitude, a relationship, or another comfort.

What is God calling you to leave? Allow God to shake up your life.

Week 32

Today, I praise God for: _____

Read Genesis 12:10–20.

We have a problem around our house that often raises its head. It goes something like this: "Daddy, Whitley just _____ (fill in the blank)." Addison likes to help with our parenting, often pointing out things Jennifer and I see Whitley doing with our own eyes, things that do not elicit a response from either of us, but "thanks" to Addison's watchful eye are pointed out. This scenario usually ends with Addison being reminded she is not the parent, and we do not need her help!

I wonder how often God needs to remind us He does not need our help?

Abram, the man who trusted God for the unknown, struggles to trust God for daily bread. There was a famine in the land, and Abram was afraid he would starve. So he went to Egypt. It was a good plan in his eyes because he knew he would be able to survive in Egypt. But it appears Abram intended to be in Egypt long term. Just as his father stopped short (Genesis 11:31–32), Abram is content to not reach the land God promised.

Approaching the borders of Egypt, Abram looks at his wife, Sarai, and is reminded of her beauty. He devises the plan to tell the Egyptians she is his sister. He was afraid they would kill him in order to take her if they knew she was his wife. Again, Abram was willing to leave his homeland to follow the Lord, but he was not willing to trust Him for physical protection.

There are times when we see an escape and take it, not because it is what God wants, but because it makes sense. We take things into our own hands because we feel God needs some help. We may not actually think that or say it, but our disobedience demonstrates it.

God will demonstrate again and again His ability to overcome obstacles and resolve jeopardy as He fulfills promises and provides what we need.

Confess where have you not trusted God to provide and enacted your own plans.

Week 33 ⟨⟩

Today, I praise God for: _____

Read Genesis 15.

A representative of the gas company phoned the owner of an expensive new home to make an appointment for the serviceman to come in to light the pilot lights and adjust the furnace. The owner stated he would have to be home in order for the serviceman to ever get the furnace going. The caller insisted his people were well trained and would have no trouble. The owner finally said, "You do not understand. When your man tries to adjust the furnace, he will go out of his mind. The thermostat in the entry hall is a dummy. It is there for my wife to play with; only I know where the real one is hidden!"

There are times in our lives when we feel like somebody has hidden the thermostat from us. These are times when we feel powerless, and we hate it. We have the promise in Romans 8:28 that "we know that all things work together for good to them that love God, to them who are called according to His purpose." Sometimes, though, we get the feeling all things are not working together for good. That can be frustrating.

That is pretty much how Abram felt. There was a war from which he had to rescue Lot. He continues to have in the back of his mind the promise that God would make him the father of many nations, but Abram wonders how the fulfillment of any promises is possible without the basic building block of a son.

Abram learned a basic lesson every believer has to learn: God's delays are not denials. God always faithfully carries out His grand plan. Even when we do not see it, or when it appears to have been forgotten, God will see His promise through to the end.

Abram waited twenty-five years for God to give him a son. The nation of Israel waited centuries for a Messiah. When we wait for God, the wait can be long, but it is more than worth it.

As you pray, be honest with God about the areas where you struggle to wait, pleading for Him to help you trust that He will keep His word.

Week 34

Today, I praise God for: _____

Read Genesis 16:1–5.

Ten years before, God promised to make Abram's descendants as numerous as the stars, but Sarai bore him nothing. Time was running out for parenthood to be a human possibility. Sarai felt the aches of old age, as did Abram, and she got to the point where she did not believe that God could do something supernatural.

Sarai could not wait on God's timing, so she devised a plan for Abram to have a child with Hagar. In this culture, this was not wrong. It was common for a husband to have a contract with his wife that stated if she could not conceive, she would find someone for her husband who could.

While socially it was not something Abram was forbidden to do, spiritually it was another matter. God had promised him a child with Sarai, and Abram believed that his offspring would be as numerous as the stars. God established a covenant with Abram, but he let his wife talk him into doing something he knew he should not be doing.

A man had a fine canary whose song was unusually beautiful. During the summer, it seemed a shame to keep the bird inside the house all the time, so the owner placed the cage in a nearby tree for the bird to enjoy the sunshine and fresh air. Many sparrows frequented the tree and were attracted to the cage. The canary was frightened at first but soon enjoyed his companions. Gradually, though, he lost the sweetness of his song. By the end of the summer, his "singing" was little more than the twitter of the sparrows. He had lost his finest song.

Peer pressure is real today. Prisons are full of people who let someone else talk them into doing something they knew was wrong. How often have your friends, spouse, or someone else talked you into doing something that caused you to compromise what you know you should be doing spiritually?

Confess where you have let someone talk you into doing something you know you should not do. Ask the Lord to strengthen you to face peer pressure.

Week 35

Today, I praise God for: _____

Read Genesis 22:1–8.

It is a directive given by many parents through the years: "Now!" An order has been given, and the children might plan on following through, but their timing is not as quick as the parents intended. Therefore, one more word is necessary to quicken the pace: "Now!"

I believe we could look at any instance in our life where God has called and add the same directive. Genesis 22 is one of my favorite passages in the Bible, and one of the things it teaches is the necessity to act quickly when God calls.

Abraham is told by God to sacrifice Isaac, the son he longed for, who probably is now a young teenager. It goes without saying that Abraham is distraught. To his credit, he ignored his feelings of anguish and grief and acted quickly on what God called him to do.

When God called Abraham, he responded with, "Here I am," a sign of trust and willingness. That trust and willingness did not change once he knew what God wanted him to do. The author gives a lot of extra details in verse 3 to give us a sense of the agony Abraham endured. He never shared this with anyone; instead, he acted quickly in his obedience to God.

God did not give Abraham a time frame for carrying out this command. I guess he could have stalled and waited days, weeks, months, or even years to follow through. Abraham realized, though, that the more time that elapsed, the less likely he was to respond to God's call.

A lesson I have learned in life is that delayed obedience is disobedience. Whenever you get a call from God, do not drag your feet. Act quickly!

What has God called you to do that you have not responded to? You cannot properly lead your family until you are obedient in this area. Commit to respond today with trust and willingness to His call on your life.

Week 36 ⟨⟩

Today, I praise God for: _____

Read Genesis 22:9–10.

I am sure Abraham longed for God to interrupt before he and Isaac, "reached the place God had told him about." He might have thought along the way, *Okay, God, you see that I am willing. I have proved that to You, so go ahead and keep me from killing my son, the one you promised me for many years.* When no miraculous intervention occurred, he had to follow through.

Can you imagine the pain Abraham felt? The bewildered look in his son's eyes. Thinking about the screams and cries of agony his son would let loose when the knife was plunged into his heart. Who could stand this torture?

This was the hardest thing Abraham ever had to do in his life, but he followed through, even when it hurt. It was excruciating, but Abraham was obedient.

We live in a time when convenience drives our decisions. When something threatens our security or comfort, we stop and count the costs. We make ourselves feel good because we intended to be obedient; it just cost too much. When it comes to faith, good intentions count for squat. God's concern is whether our faith follows through whenever He calls.

I often wonder what Isaac was thinking during this time? We know he wondered about the location of the sacrifice (verse 7), but then he was willing to lie down and be bound on the altar. They had just built it, so he knew its purpose. I am convinced that because Abraham trusted God, Isaac trusted his father. He, too, was willing to follow through, even if it hurt.

Where has pain caused you to not follow through as God called you? It may be persecution, lack of time, being tired, or many other pains, but you did not follow through. Confess this to the Lord, and commit to pick up where you left and follow through.

Do you model a trust in God that teaches your children to trust Him? Or do you believe you can stop being obedient when it hurts?

Week 37

Today, I praise God for: _____

Read Genesis 22:11–14.

Some people suffer from generalized anxiety disorder (GAD). People with GAD constantly live the fear of consequences; it is a pointless fear, based on what might happen but seldom does. They feel threatened much of the time, even when no actual threat exists.

There are times when we suffer from a spiritual version of GAD. What causes us to have fear and other feelings when God calls us to do something uncomfortable? Do we fear He is going to let us down? Do we fear life will never be sweet again? Do we wonder if God is really good after all? Simply, we lack complete trust in God.

Radical faith, tough faith, is revealed when we get past our feelings and hand the consequences over to God. Abraham had no idea what was going to happen, but he knew God would provide. He knew God was in control. He knew God is good and seeks our very best. He was able to surrender control because of his faith.

God did indeed provide. What joy there must have been at the sight of that ram caught in the bushes! Only people who take their feelings out of the driver's seat of life and put faith in control know the exhilaration of seeing God's promises fulfilled.

Abraham's test was done for God's benefit, according to verse 12.

It allowed Abraham to demonstrate to himself, to Isaac, to the world, but most of all to God that his faith was not driven by what he would receive out of it but by his commitment to God. He is willing to give up all he stands to gain, all he loves, all he hopes. That is why when God called the second time, Abraham still responded with, "Here I am." He remained willing and trusting of God's plan.

As you pray, ask God to help you trust Him so you can experience His control over the consequences of our faith.

Week 38

Today, I praise God for: _____

Read Genesis 29:14–30:24.

One day Linus and Charlie Brown were walking along and chatting with one another. Linus says, "I don't like to face problems head-on. I think the best way to solve problems is to avoid them. In fact, this is a distinct philosophy of mine. No problem is so big or so complicated that it can't be run away from!"

Jacob's family had some problems they chose to run from. Generational sin was evident throughout the family line. Jacob was a momma's boy and got her to help him trick his father into giving him the birthright that belonged to Esau, the oldest son. When Jacob was a young man, he fell in love with Rachel, the beautiful daughter of a Laban. Jacob made a deal that he would work for Laban for seven years in return for Rachel. On Jacob's wedding day, Laban pulled a switch and tricked Jacob into marry Leah, Rachel's older and less-attractive sister. Jacob agreed to work seven more years for the right to marry Rachel.

During the second set of seven years, Leah bore Jacob seven children, and he had four sons with his wife's maids. There was a lot of competition in this house, and it continued because Jacob refused to address the problem. Jacob later deceives Laban and leaves him, continuing the cycle of sin.

Later, one of Jacob's daughters was raped. Her brothers killed all the men in the city where the rape occurred and carried off all their wealth, along with their children and women. Reuben, one of Jacob's sons, later has sexual relations with Bilhah, one of his father's concubines, who was the mother of two of his half-brothers.

All this and more shows the deception, intrigue, anger, rebellion, rivalry, and out-of-control jealousy that ran rampant within the ranks of Jacob's family—all of which had been displayed by their father and grandfather.

Consider your family; what generational sins are prevalent and need to be addressed and stopped by you?

Week 39

Today, I praise God for: _____

Read Genesis 37:1–11.

One of the most prevalent sins of the family today is passivity, which is defined as a "lacking in energy or will; accepting or allowing what happens or what others do without active response or resistance." We have bought into that mind-set; we believe it is permissible to do nothing. Jacob models passivity for us.

Jacob was a passive father. He was too busy, too preoccupied and unconcerned, which meant he was too passive to deal with what was occurring in the lives of his children. As you read last week, there were many things that needed to be addressed. And then Joseph comes along and is an antagonist to his brothers. "His father kept the matter in mind." In other words, he thought about it and decided to do nothing.

Earlier, when Dinah was raped and Jacob's sons responded, Jacob was most concerned about his public relations with the rest of the people in the land. Hearing about Reuben's encounter with Bilhah, Jacob was so passive that he did nothing about it. Over and over again, Jacob seemed to fold his arms and look the other way.

Passivity is an enemy! I see many of the characteristics of Jacob in families today, as parents (and grandparents) choose to look the other way rather than address an issue. Even in Christian families, drug and alcohol abuse is rampant, especially among prescription drugs. In our passivity, we choose to believe the excuses a person offers, rather than addressing the misuse.

Families within our churches are engaged in sex outside of marriage, hatred builds against those unlike us, parents neglect the spiritual development of their children, debt is about to swallow us, children demonstrate a lack of respect for authority, and the list could go on. Rather than addressing these sins, we show our passivity and turn our heads on these issues, even making excuses for the sin.

As the Lord convicts of passivity in your life, repent and commit to address the sins and situations that are under your influence.

Week 40

Today, I praise God for: _____

Read Genesis 37:12–36.

The Harvard Business School interviewed five hundred of its graduates, all executives in large businesses. More than four hundred of them questioned their own success and brought up the name of at least one other peer they felt was more successful. Many of these individuals are considered the best and the brightest in their fields, yet they are trapped by their jealousy.

When it is allowed to grow and fester, jealousy leads to devastating consequences. It will eventually manifest itself in detrimental ways, which is what happened in Jacob's family.

Jacob did nothing to hide his favoritism of Joseph. He put it on display by giving Joseph an ornate robe, which was a sign of nobility in that day. This was a sleeved garment that extended to the knees. You cannot work in such a garment; it would be like sending a welder to a construction site wearing a full-length mink coat. Joseph probably wore it everywhere he went, including when he went to check on his brothers, who were tending the flocks. The brothers were performing hard labor in the heat when Joseph came in his coat, a sign that reminded them he did not have to work like they did.

As the saw Joseph coming, the jealousy of his brothers, combined with their anger, resulted in a plan to kill him. Judah talked some sense into his brothers, leading them to sell Joseph as a slave for a few ounces of silver.

Joseph's brothers did not get up that morning planning to get rid of their brother, but as their jealousy built that day, it led them to make an ungodly choice. Refusal to deal with jealousy will eventually be made public through our ungodly actions.

Where is jealousy evident in your life? Are you jealous of someone's job, their family, or the stuff they have? Are you jealous of a family member who received more attention than you? Repent and cherish what you have in the Lord.

Week 41

Today, I praise God for: _____

Read Genesis 39.

In the 1980s, First Lady Nancy Reagan popularized the slogan, "Just Say No!" It was used in antidrug education programs around the nation. It was a simple and straightforward response. Yet that little two-letter word can still be a difficult choice to make. Sometimes the only thing standing between you and a life-altering decision is whether you can say no to temptation.

Joseph was able to say no to Potiphar's wife multiple times as she made sexual advances toward him. Joseph is a single man in his late twenties, and the invitation from this lady happened daily. But he refused.

One day he came into the house, and it was quiet. There were no other servants about, and Potiphar's wife made her move. This time, she would not take no for an answer. She went beyond verbal advances and physically grabbed hold of Joseph. She held on so tightly that when he jerked away from her and dashed out into the street, he left his outer robe in her hands.

Whenever the New Testament touches the subject of sensual temptation, it gives one command: run! The Bible does not say to reason with it. It does not tell us to think about it and claim Bible verses will help. It tells us to flee! You cannot yield to sensuality if you are running away from it. Run for your life! If you try to reason with or play around with your thoughts, you will finally yield. That is why the Spirit of God forcefully commands, "Run!"

As we battle temptation, our emotions will plead for satisfaction. Consider the following anonymous quote: "You cannot play with the animal in you without becoming wholly animal, you cannot play with falsehood without forfeiting your right to truth, nor play with cruelty without losing your sensitivity to mind. He who wants to keep his garden tidy does not reserve a spot for weeds."

What temptations are you currently facing but are not fleeing? If you think about them, accept the warning that you are close to committing the sin you ponder. Flee from the temptation today.

Week 42 ⌣⟶

Today, I praise God for: _____

Read Genesis 40.

There is a Ziggy cartoon where he, with his big nose and bald head, stands on a mountain and gazes far above. The sky is dark, and there is one lonely cloud up there. Ziggy yells, "Have I been put on hold for the rest of my life?"

We have all felt Ziggy's pain. "Lord, will you ever answer?" How often the heavens seem more like cold brass than the place of God. We cry out, but nothing comes in return. When a dungeon experience comes, the quickest and easiest response is to feel that you have been forgotten by God.

As Joseph is in the dungeon, Genesis 39:21 says, "The Lord was with him." God never left. He was *with* Joseph! Understanding that he was not alone, Joseph maintained a vital and consistent dependency with the Lord. Because of that, God used him in significant ways.

When Joseph heard the men had a problem because they had a dream and no one to interpret it, he probably had to bite his lip. Little did they know the dreamer of all dreamers was sitting in their midst. It is amazing that Joseph would want to have anything to do with dreams, since the last time he did that, he told his brothers and ended up in the pit.

Joseph told the men to tell him their dreams, after telling them he knew it was only through God that he could interpret them. Throughout all of Joseph's dungeon and waiting experience, the Lord remained first in his life. The lens of God's will stood between Joseph and his circumstances, enabling him to see God in them, to read God in them. As a result, God was able to use Joseph in the midst of difficulty.

As we face the stresses of life, we must put our complete hope and trust in the Lord.

In your current difficulties, where is your trust? In you? In someone else? In the Lord? Declare to the Lord today your trust, and surrender your attempts to change the situation.

Week 43

Today, I praise God for: _____

Read Genesis 45:1–15.

The Bible declares that children of God have the privilege of granting forgiveness to those who have wronged them. It is referred to as a "privilege" due to the reality that we forgive others out of the forgiveness God has given us.

Joseph had long forgiven his brothers for their actions that led him to Egypt. But he did not have the opportunity to convey that forgiveness until they came to Egypt in search of food to survive the famine back home. Notice that as he offered the forgiveness, he never faulted his brothers.

He invited them to come close to him (verse 4), a phrase used for coming near for the purpose of embracing or kissing someone. It was an intimate closeness Joseph desired. They had about twenty-five years of catching up to do, which verse 15 says they spent time doing. He was cordial to his brothers, demonstrating support, mercy, grace, generosity, and unselfishness. He even offered to move them to Egypt, an offer they could not refuse.

Throughout verses 5 through 9, Joseph repeatedly gives credit to God. Rather than remembering the mistreatment, Joseph understood that God's grace was greater than any hurt in life.

Attitude is so crucial in the life of a Christian. We can go through the Sunday motions, we can carry out the religious exercises, we can pack a Bible under our arms, and we can sing songs from memory, yet we can still hold grudges against the people who wronged us. In our own way, we will get back at them. But that is not God's way.

We cannot have an intimate relationship with the Lord and properly lead our families unless we genuinely forgive those who have wronged us, just as Joseph did his brothers.

As you pray, who do you need to forgive so that you can experience God's forgiveness? Make a commitment today to be obedient to the Spirit's leading in this area of your life.

Week 44

Today, I praise God for: _____

Read Exodus 3:1–4:17.

The commanding officer was furious when nine of his subordinates did not return from their weekend passes for the morning roll call. When the first one did come in, this was his story. "I had a date, lost track of time, and missed the bus back. Being determined to get in on time, I hired a cab. Halfway here, the cab broke down. I went to a farmhouse and persuaded the farmer to sell me a horse. I was riding to camp when the horse fell over dead. I walked the last ten miles and just got here." The officer was skeptical but let the young man off with a reprimand. Then seven other men came in with the same story—had a date, missed the bus, hired a cab, bought a horse, horse fell dead, walked the last ten miles.

By the time the ninth man reported, the commander had grown weary of the story. "What happened to you?" he growled. "Sir, I had date and missed the bus back, so I hired a cab." "Wait!" the commander screeched, "Don't tell me the cab broke down." "No sir," replied the soldier, "The cab did not break down. It was just that there were so many dead horses in the road, we had trouble getting through!"

You probably have a crazy story of coming up with an excuse to get away with something or to keep from doing something. We do that spiritually, but why?

I believe we forget our encounter with God. As the first part of Exodus 3 records, Moses experiences an unusual encounter with God through a bush that burns without being consumed. Moses gets a crash course in holy etiquette as God calls him to remove his sandals. Later, Moses hides his face.

God gives Moses the plan: "I am sending you to Pharaoh to bring my people the Israelites out of Egypt." Up to this point, God has been the one doing the talking, so how will God's chosen messenger respond? He begins making excuses. Moses had gotten over his encounter with God. Similarly, when God calls us to service and we make excuses, we have forgotten about our encounter with Him.

As God convicts you of disobedience to His call, repent of your excuses, and remember your encounter with the Lord when He called you.

Week 45 ⟨⟩

Today, I praise God for: _____

Read Joshua 1.

One summer night during a severe thunderstorm, a mother was tucking her small son into bed. She was about to turn the light off when, in a trembling voice, he asked, "Mommy, will you stay with me all night?" The mother smiled, gave him a warm, reassuring hug, and said tenderly, "I can't dear. I have to sleep in Daddy's room." A long silence followed as she moved toward the door. At last it was broken by a shaky voice saying, "That big sissy."

Fear constantly lurks in the background of our lives, and there are times when it is right in front of us. For Joshua, fear was right in front of him as he was about to lead millions across a river that was at flood stage.

Perhaps for a moment, Joshua recalled a mob scene a generation ago, the panicked voices of his fellow ten spies, and the people wanting to kill Joshua and Caleb. Joshua is told three times to "be strong and courageous," meaning "unshakably courageous." This is not a manly strength or courage but a strong and courageous faith centered in the Word of God and His presence with His children.

God's command to Joshua to be strong and courageous can be fulfilled because Joshua would not be alone. Without the presence of God, Joshua had everything to fear—stiff resistance, humiliating defeat or retreat, lost confidence in his leadership, and rebellions within Israel's ranks. The presence of God, though, empowered him to lead with boldness, conviction, and confidence.

God's presence is irrevocable, as the Lord promises to never "leave" (literally "relax efforts") or "forsake" ("desert") Joshua. The Lord's efforts on his behalf will always be vigorous, His presence always constant.

We have the assurance of the Lord's presence with us today, although we face many dangers and live with many fears. Allow God's presence to banish your fears and lead you to action.

Week 46

Today, I praise God for: _____

Read Judges 6.

When Addison was born, I remember feeling so ill-equipped for the responsibilities of caring for a child. I had never changed a diaper. When I held other kids and they started crying, I gave them back to their parents. Now I had a child of my own I had to pacify. There were many times I thought, *I hope this does not kill her!*

There are times when we have that feeling spiritually. God has saved us, worked in our lives, given us the desire and ability to serve Him, but we doubt God can truly use someone like us. We get the sense that we are unqualified. Gideon understood that sentiment.

When the Lord came to Gideon, he was in a secluded area, hiding from the Midianites while he beat out the wheat in a wine press. The angel called Gideon a "mighty warrior," and instructs him that the Lord is with him. But Gideon focused on his inability rather than on the God who could do all things.

What we know most about Gideon is his fleece, but it was not the first time he asked God for a sign. Notice verse 17. Gideon had a pattern of refusing to follow God the first time He called.

Contrary to popular interpretation, these fleecings have nothing to do with discovering God's will. The divine will is perfectly and absolutely clear in Gideon's mind, as we see in verse 36. These "signs" reveal his lack of faith. No character receives more divine assurance than Gideon, and none displays more doubt. Gideon is the only judge to whom God speaks, but this privilege does not reduce his fear.

Despite being clear about God's will, being empowered by the Spirit, and seeing the response of his countrymen to lead them to battle, Gideon used every means available to try to exit the mission to which he was called.

Where do you need to quit asking God for a sign and follow His revealed will for your life?

Week 47

Today, I praise God for: _____

Read 1 Samuel 1:1–2:2.

Much has been made of Hannah's commitment to return her cherished child, Samuel, to the Lord. She was only able to do that because she had given herself to the Lord. In a pagan society, she remained steadfast in her commitment to the Lord. In her prayer, after she has kept her commitment and is leaving her toddler son, she rejoices in the Lord and His salvation.

She called the Lord her "horn," which is a symbol of strength. It is also the symbol of royal dignity. She also called God her Rock, a strong fortress, the One she relied on during the taunts of Peninnah. As she exalted the might and power of the Lord, these are not just words; they reflect her heart and who God was to her.

Jesus told the story of two men who built homes, one upon the sand and one upon the rock. The storm came and destroyed the house on sand, but the house on the rock stood strong (Matt. 7:24–27). The purpose of Jesus' parable was to lead us to build our lives on the firm foundation of the Rock, which is Christ.

Hannah built her life on the Rock. She knew there was no firmer foundation. She was an example of worship to her son because she had a personal relationship with God that fueled her trust, commitment, and life.

It is one thing to make a commitment to the Lord before you have what it takes to keep the commitment. It is another to keep the commitment when you have what it takes. Hannah commits her child to the Lord before she had a child. Once Samuel is born and she became attached to him, I am sure there was temptation to back out of the commitment. However, Hannah keeps her commitment, giving the child to the work of the Lord because her life was built on the faithfulness of God.

Do you have any commitments you made to God that you have not kept? Is He the strength and Rock of your life? If He is, then rely on Him to fulfill your commitments.

Week 48

Today, I praise God for: _____

Read Nehemiah 1.

When I drive through my hometown, I notice many changes that have occurred since the days when I kept the streets hot. Some of the changes are positive, such as new businesses and homes. Other changes are negative, as I see homes that are no longer given proper care, some businesses have closed, and I might see someone standing outside whose health has deteriorated. The negative changes often leave me disappointed and burdened.

Nehemiah had a strong love for Jerusalem, although he had the prestigious job of being cupbearer to King Artaxerxes. He was living in a fortified city when he greeted by some close associates from home. What followed reveals Nehemiah's heart. His people, the Israelites, had survived the Babylonian captivity and returned to Jerusalem, but they were in "great trouble and disgrace." The city was defenseless.

Nehemiah had a concern for others, and when he heard things were bad, he responded in a personal way- he sat and wept. "For some days" may have been three of four months, as he mourned, fasted, and prayed. When we mourn, we know our hearts are broken; when we fast and pray, we know we have become deeply involved and concerned.

Nehemiah's burden became overwhelming as he began to realize God wanted to use him to bring deliverance. He eventually went to the king and asked for permission, then resources, to return to Jerusalem to coordinate the rebuilding of the walls to fortify the city.

Nehemiah exhibited brokenness over the situation at Jerusalem. He did not just feel bad, he was broken, which always leads to action.

Where does God need to break your heart? Is it over the condition of your home, family, friends, coworkers, or classmates? Pray for brokenness. It always leads to a response to the situation.

Week 49 ⌣⟶

Today, I praise God for: _____

Read Nehemiah 4.

Discouragement can take any of us at any time. Charles Spurgeon, called "the Prince of Preachers," rarely got out of bed on Mondays due to discouragement from the previous day's ministry.

A common obstacle that keeps us from spiritual effectiveness is discouragement. We have a strong desire to serve the Lord and be used by Him, but something happens that sidetracks us, and we get discouraged. You might even be discouraged as you attempt to lead your family to observe the family altar regularly.

Nehemiah put a plan in place to accomplish the work God had for him, but he knew there would be discouragement. Sanballat and Tobiah do not let him down, as they show up to ridicule the work being done. Even though the adversity was real and the circumstances seemed too much for the Israelites to succeed, God was shown as greater and more powerful than their adversity. Nehemiah simply reminded the people of how powerful God was and told them to stand their ground.

The people complained about the rubble in verse 10. Wasn't the rubble there in the beginning? Of course it was. The difference was when they started the project, they were focused on God and His character. Now they had become rubble-gazers. If you focus on the junk in your life and in the lives of others, you will become discouraged. Commit to be God-gazers instead of rubble-gazers.

When you are down, turn your attention to the One who is able to do something about your discouragement. God has been faithful to you in the past. He is faithful to you today, and He has promised to be faithful in the future. Remember the Lord, remember His promises, remember His goodness, remember His power. He is great and awesome. Remember Him.

If you are discouraged, turn your attention from the rubble to the Lord. Realize your adversity is never greater than our God!

Week 50

Today, I praise God for: _____

Read 1 Samuel 13:1–15.

I hate to wait. When someone is supposed to be somewhere at a set time, I do not like waiting for the person to arrive late. And nothing is worse than watching the time tick down on the microwave! If you think a minute is not long, wait for that minute to pass as you wait on lunch to cook.

Life is composed of waiting periods. The child must wait until he is old enough to have a bicycle, the young woman until she is old enough to drive a car, the medical student must for her diploma, the husband for his promotion, the young couple for savings to buy a new home. The art of waiting is not learned at once.

Saul had not learned the art of waiting, and it caused him to lose the anointing of God upon his life. Saul and his men were about to engage the Philistines in battle. Samuel was supposed to arrive on the seventh day to offer the sacrifices on behalf of Saul and his men. When day seven arrived and Samuel had not arrived, Saul offered the sacrifice, mainly because, "all the troops with him were quaking with fear."

Right after Saul finished, Samuel arrived. It was still the seventh day, but he apparently did not arrive as early as Saul expected. Saul instituted his own plan, something Samuel called, "a foolish thing."

Waiting is a spiritual issue, and Saul had to wait for Samuel. But he did not. He paid the consequences for his impatience, as he was no longer God's choice to lead God's people. Isaiah 40:31 reads, "But those who wait on the Lord will find new strength. They will fly high on wings like eagles. They will run and not grow weary. The will walk and not faint."

How are you at waiting for the Lord? As He convicts of areas where you have gotten ahead of Him, instituting your own plan, repent so that revival can come to your life. Wait on the Lord, so you will find strength.

Week 51

Today, I praise God for: _____

Read 1 Samuel 21:1–9.

When the heat is on, we often act in ways that are not characteristic of us, and David was no different. He was on the run from Saul in order to save his own life and began a series of lies.

Up to this point in his life, David has been stellar, spotless, stainless. He stayed calm when his brothers snapped; he remained strong when Goliath roared; he kept his cool when Saul lost his. Now he blatantly and convincingly lied. Saul had not sent him on a mission. He was not on secret royal business. He was a fugitive, and he lied about it.

David asked Ahimelech for some food. The priest had some bread, but it was holy bread. The holy bread was placed on the table as an offering to God. After a week, the priests, and only the priests, could eat the bread. David was no priest, and the bread has just been placed on the altar. David manipulated the Law for personal benefit, persuading Ahimelech to give him some holy bread.

David presented another lie in verse 8. David's faith was wavering. Not too long before, the shepherd's sling was all he needed. Now the one who refused the armor and sword of Saul requested a weapon from the priest.

What has happened? David has lost his God-focus. A life of desperation has set in that caused him to lie and be afraid. Whereas in the past David relied solely on God to defeat his enemies, he now looked to the priest for a weapon. David once stood in the valley and shouted to Goliath that God's power was stronger than the sword he bore. Now David took that same sword, saying, "there is none like it."

David lost his focus. When trouble came looking for him, he left, he lied, and he languished. When he left Jerusalem, he left behind more than the city. He left behind his total trust in God. Once he stopped depending on God, he found lying much easier. Once he started lying, he started trusting himself more than he trusted God. Many people follow the same path to futility.

Search your heart, and determine if you have lost your God-focus.

Week 52

Today, I praise God for: _____

Read Isaiah 6.

Pastor and author John Piper warns of attempting to "do great things for God": "The difference between Uncle Sam and Jesus Christ is that Uncle Sam won't enlist you unless you are healthy and Jesus won't enlist you unless you are sick. What is God looking for in the world? Assistants? No. The gospel is not a help wanted ad. It is a help available ad. God is not looking for people to work for him but people who let him work mightily in and through them."

Isaiah was such a man. He encountered the Lord in the temple, "in the year that King Uzziah died." We are prone to skip over that part of the passage because we do not understand the setting. For Isaiah, this was a troubling time. Uzziah was a godly king, who was a strong military leader, as well as a person who loved the land of Israel. During this reign, the boundaries were expanded, and the nation was blessed immensely. Now, Uzziah was dead, and Isaiah was discouraged. It is often in our discouragement that God wants to work, but does He find a willing participant?

When Isaiah heard, "Whom shall I send? And who will go for us?" he responded with, "Here I am. Send me!" Isaiah knew he was in the presence of the Lord, and he had received the cleansing power of the Lord. For many, that would have been enough. Isaiah could have left the temple with his discouragement erased because of what he experienced in God's presence.

However, when Isaiah heard the call of God, he immediately responded with a willingness to go. He did not ask for any specifics; he simply was allowing God to work mightily in and through Him.

When the Lord told him the work was going to be very difficult, Isaiah did not back down. There is no one who would volunteer to do the work of God with no results—unless God is the one who issues the call. Isaiah faithfully fulfilled the call of God, setting an example for us to follow.

When God calls, how do you respond? Is it enough for you to know He speaks to you, or do you answer the call? Have you stopped because the job was tough?

Appendix 2
One Mother's Story

Michelle Ivy was one of the participants in the original project that served as the foundation for this book. At the time, her three children were all teenagers. The following is her story that she used in a training session for parents while on a mission trip to Chile.

I would like to share with you some things I have found to be helpful in raising godly children. I was not raised in a Christian home. God's parenting style was unfamiliar to me. When I became a mother, it became extremely obvious to me how much God loved me. I could not imagine loving any one person as much as I love my children. I wanted the best for them, just as our heavenly Father wants the best for us. God blesses us with children. We have a brief time to pass on His teachings and influence to them.

Raising my children is the most important thing I will ever do. No amount of money earned can be greater than teaching them to love God and to have a personal relationship with Him. If our Father in heaven loved us so much to sacrifice His only Son, is not His instruction worth following? I decided several years ago to trust God with my children. His ways are holy and perfect. He promises not to leave us or forsake us.

Two years ago, my oldest son went away from home to attend college. It was difficult to accept that I would not be with him to help him make wise, godly choices. I felt panicked as I watched him prepare to leave home. I worried that his faith would not be strong enough to guide him through the distraction of college life. Up to now I had a great deal of influence over where he was, who he was with, and what he was doing. I began to pray with urgency for God to watch over and protect him. Eighteen years did not seem like enough time to teach him to follow the path God has set for him.

The day came that I had to leave him at college, and I rambled on about not forgetting God in the excitement of this new freedom, that God was his strength, and to cling to his godly values—none of which I did while at college. He took me by the shoulders and looked me in my eyes, "Mom, I know. You raised me right."

It was at that moment I realized that I was the one who lacked faith. God promises in Proverbs 22:6, "Train a child in the way he should go, and when he is old, he will not turn from it." An unexplainable peace came over my heart. I knew that while I could not be with my son at college, God was with him. I know that God has proven that He loves him more than I love him by sending His Son to die on the cross for our sins.

Here are a few things I found to be helpful while teaching my children about God and His ways.

1. Pray with your children. Hearing you talk to God teaches them to go to Him with everything. They learn that God cares about us.

2. Attend Sunday school and church as a family. This teaches them the importance of studying God's Word and being obedient followers of Christ.

3. Family devotional time. This does not have to be difficult or take a long time. We allow everyone a turn at leading the devotion. This helps to get the children involved and they do not feel "preached to." It also helps everyone become more familiar with the Bible.

4. Model God's love at home. This can be difficult at times, especially with hectic schedules and tired parents. I have

had to humble myself and ask for forgiveness from my children. This has helped them learn to forgive others as Christ forgave us.

5. Guard their eyes and ears. Screen what television shows your children watch, video games they play, books they read, and Internet sites they visit. Also pay attention to the music they listen to.

6. Dress them modestly. Shop with your children, and explain how what we choose to wear can please or displease God.

7. Talk to your children about God's worldview. Discuss what the Bible says about honesty, sexual purity, alcohol and drugs, abortion, homosexuality, and marriage. Some of these topics are uncomfortable to discuss, but if parents do not teach them God's view, then they will easily be influenced by what the world considers permissive. Discussing these topics will also help you grow as a believer because you will have to study and be familiar with the Bible.

8. Seek advice from other godly parents. Many times we think we are the only ones to be confronted with a crisis. Then we discover that others have had similar experiences. Wise counsel is priceless. Be an encourager to other parents who are trying to raise their children in God's light.

I am far from being the perfect Christian parent, and my children are not perfect either. What I find most encouraging is that God does not want "perfect" people; He wants people who are teachable and obedient to His ways.

Trust God with your children; He has proven His ways are perfect.

Printed in the United States
By Bookmasters